Kicking Bear Mustangs Presents

BASIC HORSE TRAINING

Michael Hockemeyer

Basic Horse Training

Published by Hats Off Books®
610 East Delano Street, Suite 104
Tucson, Arizona 85705 U.S.A.
www.hatsoffbooks.com

International Standard Book Number: 1-58736-541-3
Library of Congress Control Number: 2005931682

CONTENTS

- III -

Riding

INTRODUCTION

When you've worked with horses for as long a time as I have, you encounter a variety of experiences. When I started, I bought all the books, all the videos, and went to many training demonstrations. I tried to learn from the experience of others, hoping I could find a shortcut to becoming a great trainer. This book is the result of what I've learned.

I quickly learned that most books and videos were great at showing you both point A and point C, but Point B was almost never covered. In other words, there was always a lot of discussion on getting the horse haltered and rubbed down. Then the lessons would jump almost immediately to riding. There was always a gap in between. This makes it very hard to learn. In fact, I found myself buying books that were hundreds of pages long and getting some type of benefit from only five pages. The rest of the book was a mystery to me. Either the lessons applied to advanced riding styles that went beyond what the average rider needs or the book was filled with philosophy, and flowery stories about training horses. Don't get me wrong, philosophy is important. However, it takes sweat and ingenuity to train a horse. Experience has been my best teacher.

I soon began training horses for other people. For a comparatively small fee, I'd go to the person's house and train their horse. I had good results with the horses when the owners sometimes did not. I found out quickly that even though I asked them to watch me and then work with their horses on their own, most people wouldn't—

not because they didn't care, but because they didn't understand everything that was happening in the lessons. I realized that this was mostly my fault and that I had to do something to remedy that problem. I started writing my lessons down on paper, with a few sketches thrown in to help explain things. The response was great. I tried to keep the lessons simple and basic so they wouldn't confuse even beginners. Before I knew it, I had a whole bunch of lessons—enough to put this book together.

These lessons have come from my experience. They're all things I do while I train my own horses. Each horse is a little different, and these lessons won't give you every answer, but they'll give you a good place to start. Remember, experience is the best teacher. These lessons were written to give you a bit of my own experience, something to guide you in the right direction toward your own experiences. I've kept the flowers out of this book. There are no long stories about the philosophy behind horses and horse riding. This is a complete training book that will take you from point A to point C *without* skipping over B.

So sit back and then, when you're ready, throw it into a bag and head for the barn. The lessons are step by step, so don't be afraid to take the book with you so you can refer to it on the spot. Take your time and use my experience to help you learn about your horse. Keep an open mind, and you'll soon gain plenty of your own experiences to learn from.

Good luck!

1

Basic Ground Training

1

LUNGING

There are many ways to start a horse. I begin with *lunging*. Lunging is more than just an exercise. It's more than just mindless circles. Lunging is a good way to determine who's in charge. The horse should learn that *you* decide when it's time to move, and *you* decide when it's time to stop. Your horse should learn that *you* decide in which direction it should be moving. Also, you should learn how much motivation you'll need to give your horse in order to get those responses. All of it can be done without a rope or halter, and in the end, both of you should be aware of your places in your small herd of two. All of that comes from lunging.

I begin with lunging because it's safe. Lunging allows me the opportunity to work the horse without having to get too close. In a small round pen, about thirty feet in diameter, I can safely work a horse and influence its movements while both of us respect each other's boundaries. As with all horse activities, safety is a priority.

Spend time lunging. It's relatively easy on the both of you and yields great benefits. For a horse that starts with a lot of unfocused energy, lunging is a way to channel that excitement. For a horse that's untrained, it's a good way to establish who leads and who follows. Future exercises, like mounted turns, are influenced by lunging, and it can also be a good means of reprimanding when a horse loses focus. Horses prefer to stand still and rest, but with lunging, they're forced to move. Lunging affects a number of horse activities, so spend some time to get it right.

Keep in mind that lunging is also the horse's first job. It's amazing how this one thing can change a horse's attitude. It gives the horse a purpose when it's with you. Think about the first job you ever had— that first *real* job before you realized how terrible it can be to work nine to five. I know I felt as if I suddenly was serving a purpose. The responsibility of having a job made me feel important and grown up for the first time. It's the exact same way for a horse.

When a horse lunges correctly for the first time, you'll see a whole new horse. You'll see a confidence that might not have been there before. That attitude should never leave the horse from that point on—and it all begins with lunging.

The first step in lunging is to get the horse moving—let's say to the left.

1. While facing the horse, extend your left arm as if to point the way. With your right hand, either wave a rope or your hand to create a stimulus to get the horse moving. As the horse begins to move, keep your left hand extended to *lead* the horse. Continue to *drive* the horse with your other hand.

2. When you want the horse to stop, you want it to turn and face you. This will put you in a safe position, and get the horse in a good position to follow your next cue. When you want the horse to stop, lower your leading hand and take one step back and away from the horse. The idea is to take all the pressure off of it and get it to watch you. If the horse doesn't turn to face you, take another step back and away. Eventually the horse will have to turn just so it can keep an eye on you.

3. Once it turns, stop and position yourself toward the horse's front again. Each time you practice this step, it will get easier for both of you.

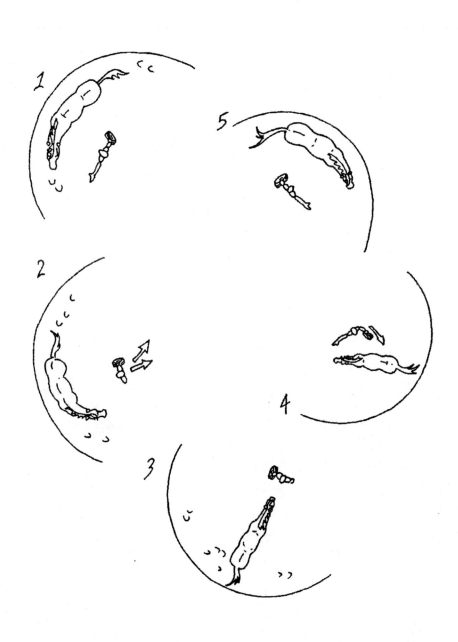

4. When you're ready, direct the horse to move in the opposite direction. That means your right arm will be the leading arm, while your left becomes the driving arm.

5. As the horse moves, keep your leading arm extended, and use your driving arm to keep the horse moving.

Lunging can be done with a rope around the horse's neck, or with a rope attached to the halter. If you're beginning with a wild or very nervous horse, I recommend doing this a few times with nothing on the horse. Sometimes a rope can cause more problems than it's worth. Working in a round pen or small paddock will help keep the horse's attention focused on you.

As you lunge the horse, pay attention to every movement *both* of you make. Every gesture carries an importance. Focus on the connection that you're creating. I often find that in the beginning of a horse's lesson, both the horse and I are tense and working in opposing directions. Through lunging, we begin to feel each other out. We begin to learn about each other's character.

As we learn about each other, we settle into our positions as *leader* and *follower*. As we settle into those positions, we find calm in knowing that we each have a place in the herd. As training continues, lunging becomes a point of reassurance. No matter how bad a training day goes in the future, both horse and horseperson can return to lunging. It also provides a means to assert your leadership when it comes into question, and it gives the horse a way to show that it hasn't given up hope for you yet.

2
First Touch

Touching a horse is very often an overlooked blessing. For any animal, being touched by a human is the opposite of what centuries of evolution has taught them. Touching can happen in two ways: forced or accepted. With horses, forced touching usually happens when a person ties up a horse and gives it no other option but to be touched. Although this method does work, it usually results in (at least) a few cuts and bruises for both trainer and horse. Forced touching also lacks an important ingredient to any relationship—trust.

Trust is the one thing that will get your horse to work through any problem. With trust, you'll not only be able to get your horse *out* of a burning barn, you'll be able to ride it back *into* it to save your other horses. The only way to gain trust is to get your horse to accept the idea that it's okay to let you touch it. Once it realizes that you aren't going to force it and you're willing to be patient, it will readily accept your touch. Working toward gaining the horse's acceptance of your touch takes more time and hard work, but it's a much safer and easier way to work with your horse. The acceptance method might not be as macho as the force method, but I guarantee it will end in less feelings of resentment from the both of you.

For safety reasons, before you start to touch the horse, we should go over some important ideas about how horses see the world. A horse uses vision, along with all its other senses, to help detect danger. Vision is one of the few aspects we can work around. In other words, we can't change our smell easily and we can't change the sound of our voice all the time, but we can change how we present ourselves physically to the horse.

The most important aspect to keep in mind is that, to a horse, humans are *predators*. Even if you've never touched a piece of meat in your life—you're still a predator. Our features give us away. We don't graze, so we have short faces and short necks. Our eyes are close together to give us good vision, with depth perception for striking at prey. Probably the most overlooked aspect is our hands. Our hands bear striking resemblance to a paw with large claws. Imagine the palm of your hand as a paw, and each of your fingers as large nails. To a horse that's always on the lookout for predators, that could easily be seen as a threat. So keep that in mind when preparing to touch the horse. Keep your fingers together so that your hand looks like one large paw without claws. Hold your hand flat so your hand doesn't resemble curved nails. Most importantly, move your hand slowly and let the horse smell it first. *Then* touch it.

Body language is also important. Body language will reflect your leadership abilities to the horse. When two horses meet for the first time, do they slouch? No. When horses meet, they look each other in the eye, keep their heads held high, and make sure the other horse sees them. At that point, they're sizing each other up. Watch a very dominant horse get introduced to a young horse sometime. Surprisingly, there's almost never any fighting. When the young horse sees the strong posture of the dominant horse, it almost immediately drop its head down and breaks eye contact. That's how important body language is to a horse. If you're going to lead, be a strong leader. Hold your head up high, make deliberate movements, and always try to keep eye contact.

Knowing how well a horse sees you is extremely important. As prey animals, their eyes are set on the sides of their heads, which gives them some unique vision qualities. Horses have a great field of vision. Each eye sees a different side of the horse. This means that the majority of what a horse sees, it sees with monocular vision.

(Monocular vision is everything you see with one eye.) That vision isn't quite as clear as ours and it doesn't give a horse depth perception. Depth perception tells you how far away an object is, which is very important when it comes to touching. For example, cover one eye and try to play catch with a friend. It won't work well.

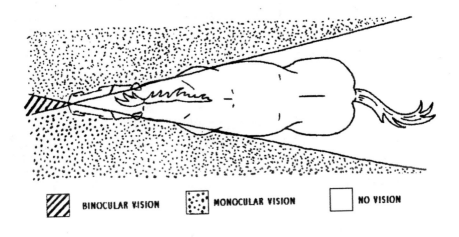

BINOCULAR VISION   MONOCULAR VISION   NO VISION

If you look at the diagram, you'll notice there's a place where the two monocular fields cross. That area is where a horse sees with binocular vision. (Binocular vision is everything you see with two eyes.) Humans have binocular vision. That vision is clearer and gives a sense of depth perception. With that vision, a horse can tell how far away you really are.

The diagram also shows that a horse has two blind spots. One is in front of the horse, directly between the eyes and has very little impact on the horse's field of vision. The other blind spot seems to be the most forgotten, yet biggest cause of injury for people. A horse can't see a thing directly behind it. Have you ever seen someone walk up behind a horse, pat it on the butt, and then get kicked? It's not because the horse didn't like that person. It was because that person startled it. Another way to startle the horse is to come from behind and then suddenly appear in its field of vision. That usually results in the horse taking a quick step or hop to the side so it can see you better. In other words, if you want to make a horse nervous, stand in its blind spot. Unless the horse has been well trained, it's not going to be happy. For some reason, that rear blind spot is always overlooked.

The most important thing you can gain from this information is an understanding of how it all affects touching a horse. The short version is: when you go to touch a horse, make sure it can see you, and even if it *can* see you coming, understand that it might not know how far away you are.

So don't be surprised if a horse is okay with your hand being a few inches away but jumps when you actually make contact. That just means that it saw your hand, but didn't realize it was that close. Once you get on a horse's back, realize that it can't see you, which is going to make the horse uneasy at first. If you're going to do anything on a horse's back, such as roping, polo, archery, western shooting, or just waving your hand to say hi, be aware that you'll suddenly be moving objects from the horse's blind spot into its field of vision, and without some prior training, the horse will probably take a few quick steps. The horse's vision contributes toward many of its reactions, so always keep this lesson in the back of your mind while you're working with horses.

The first time you're going to touch your horse, you'll probably notice that it will put you on one particular side. For now, focus heavily on that one side, since horses are right or left-handed, just like humans. It's nothing personal about you. The horse will simply put you on the side where it can kick best. After you can touch the horse on that side, try the other.

With that in mind, I begin touching at a safe distance. For this, I use a flag on a stick (a bandana on a lunging whip). The horse seems to react better to the flag at first, and it keeps both of us a safe distance from each other. Once I can easily touch the horse with the flag, I begin the same procedure, using my hands.

In this lesson, you want to work at a pace that's fast enough to show results, but not so fast as to stress the horse. I usually spend a few days just using the flag before I switch to my hands. It takes longer, but it builds a stronger foundation.

The best way to work through this lesson is using an "approach and retreat" method. Basically, you want to bring the flag (or your hand) into view and let the horse see it. Hold it in front of the horse at a distance that allows it to smell the flag without having to worry about being touched. Then move the flag away. Following that, bring the flag toward the horse again, stopping at the spot where the horse becomes noticeably nervous. Hold the flag there for a few moments and then retreat it to a safe distance. Each time you advance the flag toward the horse, bring it a little closer.

Once you finally touch the horse, don't be surprised if it gives a little jump. Remember, it could probably *see* the flag just fine—it just didn't know exactly how far away the flag was. After you've touched it once, expect the horse to be slightly apprehensive the next few times you bring the flag close. Be patient and persistent, and the horse will eventually become accepting.

When doing this exercise, there's a specific sequence I like to follow. It seems to keep the horse calm throughout the exercise and helps it prepare for the next step. As you work through this sequence, be cautious with your flag on a stick. Don't *poke* the horse, let the flag *pet* it.

1. I begin by touching the horse's lower neck, just above the shoulder. Horses seem to like starting there because they have a good view of the flag. *I* like starting there because it keeps the stick far away from the horse's eyes for that first touch. Trust me, it's all fun and games until your untrained horse gets poked in the eye and needs veterinary attention.

2. The upper neck comes next. I pay close attention to touching the top line of the neck. That's where a rope or halter will go while I'm trying to put it on, so I like the horse to know its okay to be touched there. Once I can touch that spot, I stroke down the

neck, and get the horse used to a flag or hand moving along its body.

3. Once the neck is done, I start on the face—at the forehead. The forehead is actually a great place to reward a horse. Rubbing the forehead is very soothing to a horse, for some reason. When a young horse nurses from its mother, its forehead rubs against the mare's belly. I think that's why most horses find this spot particularly sensitive to a good rub. I think it makes them feel relaxed, like when they were younger.

4. From the forehead, it's easy to pass the flag in front of the ears and down the side of the face. This is an important spot when it comes to haltering, because it's the area where you'll probably need to tie a knot or fasten a buckle.

5. It's also easy to drop the flag from the forehead to the top of the nose. Any type of halter will require you to touch the horse's nose at some point.

6. After the nose, I touch under the jaw. This spot will be stressful for the horse, because it can't see what you're doing. I generally don't push for excellence in this section at first. I just like to expose the horse to the idea of being touched there.

7. Finally, I stroke down the front of the neck, which is a dangerous spot for a horse. There are four main spots a predator will attack a horse to inflict injury: the legs (which carry the horse), the belly (which is unprotected by bone), the back (which is out of kicking range), and the neck (which is where the jugular vein is). The horse knows the front of its neck is an exposed weakness and may be very nervous about being touched there.

Touching is a big step toward breaking down the predator/prey boundary. There are very few things that will be as important or as rewarding as getting the horse to accept your touch. As you touch the horse, focus on what you're doing. Does the hair on your horse feel soft or coarse? Does the horse feel warm to the touch? Does it tense up when you touch it, or does it relax? Where are the most sensitive parts on your horse? Which parts does it seem to enjoy the most? The more you touch your horse, the more you'll learn about your horse.

3

HALTERING

Once the horse can be touched with the flag and your hands on both sides of its head and neck, you can start to think about haltering. For a wild or rough horse, I find most halters to be a little cumbersome to put on at first. For this reason, I use something else. I use a piece of rope about fifteen feet long with a loop tied in one end. This rope can be used to make a quick and easy halter that comes with its own lead line.

As with any new item, allow the horse to smell it first. Then rub the horse down with it, just like you did with the flag. You might find that you need to use the same approach and retreat method to keep the horse calm. Once it's calm with the rope you can start working toward putting it on. For a wild horse, this is never as easy as it sounds, so be patient. Wild and rough horses take time—so give them time.

1. Start by placing the looped end of the rope over the horse's neck.

2. Fold the rope and pass the new fold through the loop to construct another loop.

3. Take that new loop, and with one rub on the nose, place it over the horse's face. Pull the slack out of the line, and you have a haltered horse with a lead line!

4

TOUCHING THE FACE

Now that you have better control of the horse's head, rub the horse down thoroughly. Rub all the same places on the head and neck that you did with the flag. With the head under control, you can focus more on the face. A lot of people don't focus on the face and end up with problems. For example, by systematically rubbing the face, you can get the horse used to worming, eye treatments, ear twitches, and much more. Many people don't think about those things while training, but, believe me, your vet does.

I go through a quick sequence that takes just a few minutes. It's so quick and beneficial that I do it every day to each of my horses—even the well trained ones benefit from this exercise. With horses, it pays to pay attention to even the littlest details. Exposing them to something when it's convenient for you is easier than trying to do it when there's an urgency.

1. I always start at the forehead.

2. Next, I move to the ears, since almost all bridles require you to move the ears in some way. If you never plan to use a bridle, you might still need to do an ear twitch on your horse. (An ear twitch is when you pull the ear straight out, slightly away from the skull. It's not meant to hurt the horse, but to distract it while you give it a shot or do something else that's uncomfortable.)

3. From the ears, I move to the eyes. When I worked in a veterinary practice, I hated giving eye drops more than giving shots. Almost all horses hated having their eyes touched, which made it difficult to get medicine in their eyes. All you have to do is rub their eyes, but if you really want to be thorough, open their eyelids a little. That will make it much easier to get ointment into the horse's eyes when necessary.

4. Pick their nose. It may seem kind of gross, but it's practical. More and more vaccines are being given intranasally. That means they go into the nose instead of via a shot. If your horse begins to colic and needs mineral oil pumped into it, the vet will pass a tube down its nose. If you just stick your thumb up the horse's nostril (one at a time), you'll have a much easier time giving medicines through the nose later on.

5. The mouth is often overlooked, but by putting your thumb in the side of the horse's mouth and rubbing its gums, you'll make future worming much easier. You'll also give the horse a jump-start on taking a bit. I also like to run a finger up the inside of the cheek along the teeth. That's how you check to see if a horse needs to have its teeth floated. If you feel sharp projectiles along the teeth, your horse will probably need a little dental attention in the near future.

6. At some point, almost every horse needs to get a nose twitch put on. A nose twitch provides a distraction while you or your vet perform a more painful task. You can prepare the horse for this by gripping the tip of the nose and pulling out slightly.

All of these steps fall into a quick pattern that shouldn't take more than a few minutes. If you do it every day, you'll find it becomes a quick way to say hello to your horse. Rub its forehead, wiggle its ears, and play peek-a-boo. Pick its nose, rub its gums, and give it a big kiss on the tip of its nose as you pull on it. Most people do some of these things by accident, but you should turn it into a regular routine.

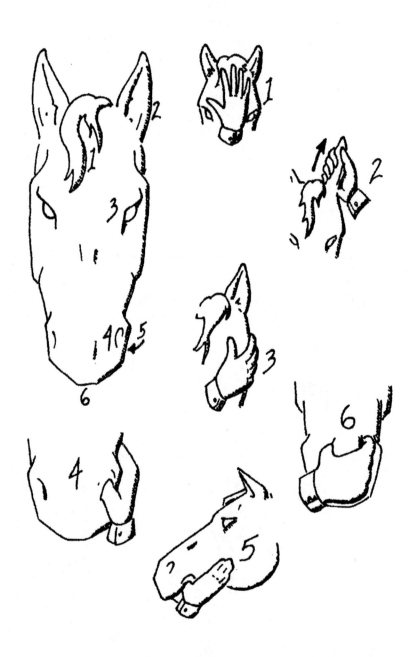

MOVING ON WITH TOUCHING

Now that the halter is on and you have better control over the head, you can start touching the rest of the body. Again, I begin with the flag, which allows me to touch the horse all the way back to its tail while remaining safely in front of the shoulder. Again, I break the body into sections. With each new major section touched, I remove the flag and give the horse a rub on the head or neck to congratulate it. Then I start again with a section I've already covered and move to a new one. I always begin from the lower neck/shoulder region until the horse is comfortable with the flag, moving the flag slowly along the horse's body and making frequent stops to congratulate it.

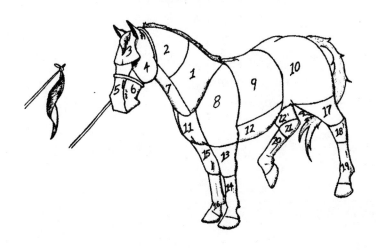

Rubbing Order:

1. Lower Neck
2. Upper Neck
3. Forehead
4. Cheek
5. Nose
6. Jaw
7. Front of Neck
8. Shoulder
9. Back
10. Rump
11. Chest
12. Stomach/Girth Area
13. Upper Arm (outside)
14. Lower Front Leg (outside)
15. Upper Arm (inside)
16. Lower Front Leg (inside)
17. Gaskin/Stifle (outside)
18. Hock (outside)
19. Lower Hind Leg (outside)
20. Lower Hind Leg (inside)
21. Hock (inside)
22. Gaskin/Stifle (inside)

I often break this exercise up even more, depending on the horse. For example, I might settle for touching the body and front legs one day, and then include the hind legs during the next session. Even if you get it all done in one day, work on it a few days more. For an unbroken horse, I do this exercise at the beginning of every session. Once the horse becomes understanding about the flag, the exercise goes very quickly and takes on a new perspective. During later training sessions, I go through the exercise quickly, to make sure the horse is ready to be touched all over before I start putting on a saddle or blanket. Don't do this exercise once and then never do it again. It's good to reinforce the exercise often. It'll be very helpful in getting the horse to accept being touched by new objects, and it's a quick way to limit the chances of any painful accidents during training.

USING A ROPE TO TOUCH

After the flag, I like to get a little closer to the horse, but not so close that I have no means of escape. For this, I use a saddle rope. (Everyone should own a saddle rope.) Even if you don't do roping, a saddle rope is a useful training tool. It's rigid, so it allows you to touch the horse with more pressure than the flag, and a saddle rope can be used later to teach the horse to pick up its feet, get it used to cinch pressure, to drag objects, and much more. In any case, a saddle rope isn't just for cowboys—it's a worthwhile addition to anyone's horse equipment.

Using a saddle rope to rub down the horse applies a new stimulus, and you can apply more pressure to spots where more pressure will be needed. For instance, you can apply pressure to the cinch and chest strap areas of the horse, which will help the horse get ready for what it will feel like when a saddle goes on and is cinched up. You can also jiggle the rope along the horse's body. When putting equipment on a horse, the equipment sometimes bumps into it in different ways, which may frighten the horse. Exposing a horse to rigid objects during the training process will help things go more smoothly in the future—and jiggling the saddle rope on the body helps.

Notice on the diagram that I don't rub low on the legs with the rope. Until the horse can have its legs lifted safely, I don't like putting my head down into kicking range. We'll get to those parts later, but for now, I don't recommend bending over to touch the lower legs.

Rubbing Order:

1. Forehead
2. Cheek
3. Neck
4. Front of Neck
5. Shoulder
6. Back
7. Side of Chest
8. Cinch Area
9. Chest
10. Rump
11. Gaskin/Stifle

FLAGGING

I don't like horses that spook easily. Horses that jump at every little movement are dangerous. Some horses are naturally inclined to behave this way in new situations. However, you can expose these horses to different things and train some of the spookiness out of them. One training method is called *slicker breaking*. It gets its name from the idea that if you were out riding and a storm came up, you should be able to put your rain slicker on without the horse going nuts. That doesn't sound too tough to someone who's never tried it while the wind is blowing that slicker all over the place, but, believe me, it can cause problems. This lesson is meant to help the horse get accustomed to objects moving all around it at varied speeds. It will also get the horse used to objects moving quickly toward it. Understand, however, that this isn't a cure-all. It's only one of many ways that you should expose your horse to different stimuli.

This exercise is done using the flag.

1. I begin in front of a haltered horse. (The lesson takes a lot longer if the horse isn't haltered.) I wave the flag in front of the horse at a distance, moving it slow at first and then moving it faster. I stop and let the horse smell the flag once or twice, then continue to wave the flag in front of the horse at a slight distance until the horse seems calm. (Note that there's a difference between *calm* and *relaxed*. A calm horse will still be very attentive to everything

you do. Its ears and eyes will be on you and the flag. A relaxed horse will look away and not pay attention, which can be dangerous if something suddenly startles the horse. I'll take an attentive, calm horse over a relaxed, somewhat sleepy horse any day.)

2. Next, I move in closer and wave the flag around the horse's head—on both sides and above. The idea is to get the horse to a point where it doesn't jerk its head around when the flag comes near. I'm careful not to poke the horse in the eyes as I wave and shake the flag, taking it out to a distance and then bringing it in to touch the horse.

3. Moving on to the rest of the body, I become creative. The more a horse gets used to a flag moving all around it, the better. I move the flag out and then bring it in to touch the horse at various speeds around the entire body.

4. I then wave the flag near the ground in front and to the sides of the horse, moving the flag along the ground as if it were being blown by the wind. I also make the flag come up from the ground and touch the horse, which gets it used to having some-

thing moving suddenly near its feet. (Who knows, one day I might have my head or foot down there!)

Once the horse can face the flag without major issues, experiment with different things. (For example, put a plastic grocery bag on the end of the stick and go through the same exercise.) I sometimes take a blanket, rub the horse down with it, and then shake it around. Get out your rain slicker and rub your horse down with it. The point is, the time you spend in the beginning to get your horse exposed to new things will shorten the time you'll spend later on the back of a stampeding, frightened horse.

As you introduce new objects, realize what else you're showing your horse. The underlying lesson being taught is about *comfort*. You may be introducing new, scary objects to your horse, but you're also helping it overcome its fears. The horse is learning that as long as you're there, nothing is going to hurt it. That doesn't mean the horse will never get scared again, but it will learn that you'll be there to comfort it when something frightens it. That will help it work through a frightening situation more calmly in the future.

True friends stand beside each other in the face of adversity. Show your horse that you can stand in front of it to lead and teach new things, and that you'll stand beside it when it needs a friend.

8

LEADING

Leading is an often-overlooked skill, but it's an extremely important one. If you're unable to lead your horse, you'll have a hard time doing any type of work with it. Horses that can't be led well usually don't like being caught when they're at pasture. They don't like to follow into new situations, and as a result, they can be dangerous. If you plan to be able to walk out into the pasture, get ahold of your horse, lead it into the barn, or put it into a trailer, your horse will need to be able to be led.

Leading isn't just a practical lesson to get work done. It's also a big step in your relationship with the horse to let it know that you're *leading* and it's *following*. This lesson will have a large impact on how your horse works with you, and will make your horse more respectful and calm during further lessons, so take your time and don't settle for a horse that isn't good at being led.

Teaching a horse to lead can be done in many ways, but there are two that I prefer. For an older or more nervous horse, I prefer a side step method. For a younger, more open-minded horse, I like to use a butt rope. Both methods work well, but the butt rope tends to go a little quicker, although it also comes with the higher possibility of accidents. Look at both methods and decide which one will be easiest for your horse. If you need to take an extra day or two with the side-step method because your horse won't tolerate a rope on its butt, *do* it.

First, let's look at the side-step method. With all horses, the idea behind leading is to get them moving, and the trick to getting them

28

moving is getting their back legs un-braced. You're probably familiar with that look. They hold their head up high, lock their legs, and put all their weight in their back end. Basically, the horse turns into a one thousand-pound statue—one that isn't going to move for *anyone*. When that happens, what should you do? After all, playing tug-o-war with a horse usually doesn't work out well for the human.

All it takes is a step to the side to get the horse to move.

Side-Step Method

1. Apply *constant* pressure on the lead line. You don't need to use all of your muscle—just enough to take the slack out of the line.

2. If the horse braces up and won't move, keep applying pressure and walk a few steps to the side. The idea is to force the horse to move in order to maintain its balance. When it's forced to turn to keep its balance, the horse will eventually have to unlock its hind legs and move. As soon as the horse moves its hind legs, stop and *relax the line*.

3. Return to your starting position in front of the horse. Again take the slack out of the line. Always give the horse the opportunity to walk forward just by applying pressure on the lead line first. If it doesn't go, take a step to the side and get it to move. With each try, you should notice that it takes less and less side pressure to get the horse to move. If you start out doing this in a round pen, that's fine, but do it in a larger paddock or corral also, because most horses react differently in more open surroundings.

I use the butt rope method for younger horses that are a little easier to push around or for calmer horses that don't mind pressure on their hind ends. This method allows me to use a rope around the butt to push the horse forward without actually getting behind it. It's a great method, but can be risky with a more nervous horse. No

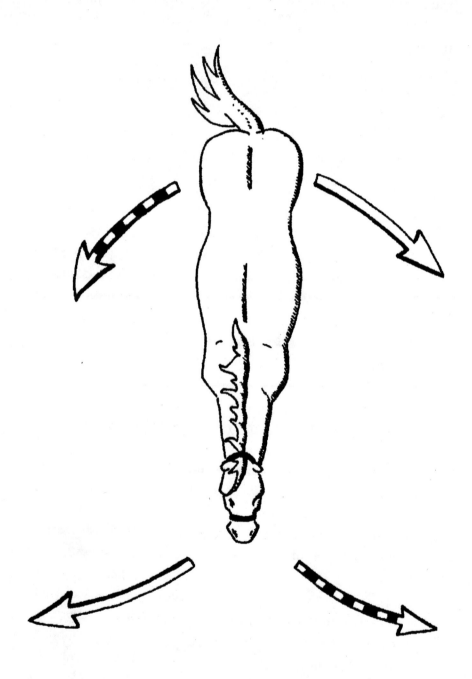

matter what the horse's temperament is, be cautious when you apply pressure on the butt rope. The rope is meant to apply enough pressure to get the horse moving, and it will sometimes get moving very quickly in your direction, so always use *caution* when attempting this method.

Butt Rope Method

1. Using a long rope with a loop at one end (a saddle rope works best), slide the rope over the horse's back so the loop rests over the majority of the butt. Be cautious not to let the rope move too far out of position. (A rope under the tail can cause a lot of chaos.) The other end of the rope should be run under the chin and through the halter, which gives you *two* lead lines.

2. To get the horse moving, apply pressure to the halter line—just enough to take the slack out of the line.

3. If the horse doesn't move, gently apply pressure to the butt line. Be ready for the horse to jump the first time or two. Once it moves, relax all pressure on the butt line.

4. Begin again, first with the halter line, and then the butt line. The idea is to use the butt line only to get the horse started. As soon as it starts walking, relax the line. If it stops again, use the butt line to get the horse going again. *Never* apply continuous pressure to the butt rope.

With the butt rope, make sure the rope doesn't slip into unwanted areas on your horse. Also make sure that the rope goes through the halter. That will help make sure that you're applying forward pressure to the rope with every pull. If you don't put the rope through the halter, you might end up pulling the butt to the side while you're trying to pull the horse forward. You also want to do

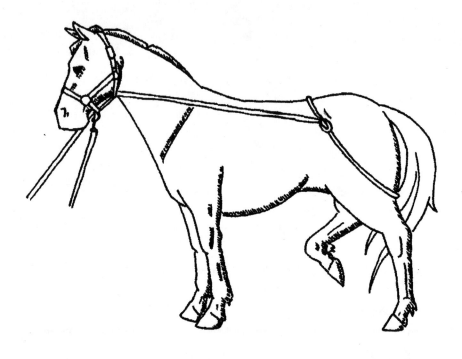

this *away from other horses*. If you're dealing with a foal, *have the mother there*. You don't want to risk having other horses get caught up in the butt rope by accident. With this method, I work in a small environment. When the horse seems to get the idea of leading, I take it out to a bigger paddock to try leading without the butt rope.

Be creative with your leading lessons. When all is said and done, you should be able to loop the lead line in your belt and lead the horse with almost no pressure. The horse should stop when you stop and start walking when you start walking. The horse should also learn to keep pace with you, which takes a little longer to teach, but the horse should learn to increase and decrease its pace as you do. I prefer horses to get to a point where I don't need to use a lead line at all. I walk, and they follow. Even if I pick up the pace to a jog, I like the horse to keep up by trotting behind. Don't just settle for your horse being "only okay" at leading.

9

BACKING

Backing is a very important skill that can be taught in several ways. Since I like to arrive at a point where I don't have to use the reins, I've adopted a particular way of teaching a horse to back, using two separate cues.

1. First, I apply mild pressure on the horse's nose by moving the lead line back toward the shoulder. This gets the horse used to yielding to pressure from the reins. As the horse moves back, I release the pressure and give it a rub on the neck.

2. As I bring the lead line toward the shoulder, I apply pressure at the front of the shoulder, as if to push the horse backward. When I ride without reins, I bring my legs forward and use my heels to pull the shoulders back. If I'm working from the ground, it's more convenient to get the horse to back by pushing on its shoulder.

I use these two methods because they make the most sense to me. I'm getting the horse to back either by pressure at the nose or pressure at the shoulder. I've seen people teach backing by shaking the lead line in front of the horse, or by waving their hands in front of the horse. That may get the horse to move back, but it's usually because it's nervous, so those methods seem impractical. For example, if you're out riding, are you going to dismount and shake the reins in front of the horse in order to get it to back up? If you do, your friends will probably laugh at you. If you are going to take the time to train your horse, do it right the first time.

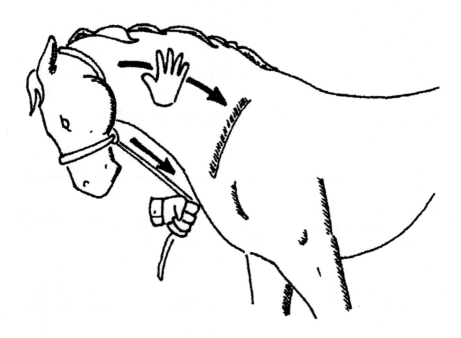

10

TURNING

Turning is where many people have the hardest time—especially while riding. I think it's because there is a lot that needs to be done in order to get a good turn. The thing I notice most is that people tend to rely only on the reins. If the horse doesn't respond, they pull harder on the reins. If the horse still doesn't respond, the rider puts a more severe bit in its mouth. However, you can turn a horse without using the reins at all. In fact, there are three major ways that a horse can know when to turn, and they can be used together or individually.

1. The reins.

2. Leg pressure.

3. Balance/Weight.

Turning by the balance/weight method is a more advanced technique, incorporating changes of *your* center of gravity in relation to your *horse's* center of gravity. This method is for faster, more advanced riding that won't be covered in this book, and isn't a method you'll routinely see employed in the show ring. It's mentioned here only to make you aware that your balance and center of gravity can be used to cause a horse to turn. As you progress in riding, always be aware of your body's movements, and understand how they affect your horse.

Reins and leg pressure are what I'll focus on in this book. Reins are easy to understand, so I'll spend some time explaining leg pressure. Leg pressure does *not* refer to kicking a horse, nor does it require spurs. Leg pressure comes very naturally—if you let it. Leg pressure is also difficult to explain, so with that in mind, let's discuss the basic ideas of turning.

Turning requires the horse to bend, and when an object bends, one side needs to contract while the other side extends. A slinky spring is a great example. If you apply pressure to one side of the spring by pushing at the center, the other side opens and expands to bend around that pressure. When you release the pressure, the spring settles back to its original position. The same idea applies to all objects—including horses. When a horse turns, one side of its body needs to stretch and extend while the other side needs to contract. Using this concept, we can expect that if we apply leg pressure to the right side of the horse, the right side will contract while the left side extends—just like the slinky spring.

Staying with the spring analogy, if you apply pressure at the ends of the spring, those ends will expand around the center. On a horse, the shoulders and hips are like the ends of the spring. While sitting in the saddle, we can't reach the hips, but we can reach the shoulders, so if we apply pressure on the right shoulder, it makes sense that the right side will extend around the left.

Using those two concepts, you can begin teaching the horse to turn from the ground. The direction of the turn will be determined by where you apply pressure. We'll begin by getting the hind end to move.

To get the hind end to go to the left:

1. Stand on the horse's right side, at the shoulder, holding the lead line in your right hand as you face the right side of the horse.

2. Place your left hand behind the horse's elbow, but don't push yet. The idea is to place your hand where your leg would be while riding.

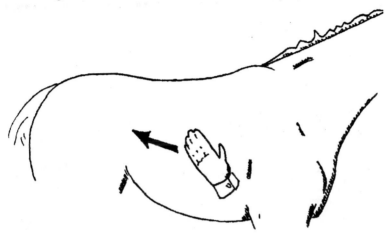

3. Begin to move your left hand back slightly, toward the middle of the rib cage. As your hand moves back, apply *constant* pressure, but don't poke at the horse's side. The idea is to get the horse used to the same type of pressure you'll be applying with your legs later.

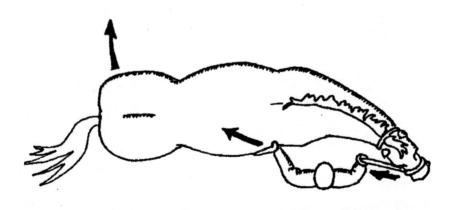

4. If the horse doesn't move after you've started applying pressure, use your right hand to put pressure on the lead. This pressure will help the horse learn to yield to rein pressure. Don't start with rein

pressure, and then leg pressure—always start with the *least severe* signal and build up from there.

5. Once the horse takes one step, *relax* and bring your hands back to the starting position to begin again.

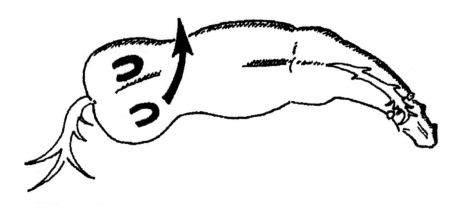

As the horse turns, it's important that it remains balanced. For this, you'll want to make sure that the horse moves its feet properly as it turns. The horse should move its inside back leg up and in front of the outside back leg. In other words, if the horse is turning its hind end to the left, the right hind leg should step up and in front of the left hind leg.

Most horses will start off by doing a *shuffle step*. A shuffle step happens when the horse doesn't take a good step in front of the other leg. It just slides the feet next to each other. When a horse does a shuffle step to the side, you'll notice that it kind of hops. This can be dangerous at faster speeds, because horses that shuffle step at high speeds can trip or fall. If your horse seems to shuffle step, ask it to turn using the described techniques above. However, don't relax until your horse takes a good, smooth step.

I've yet to meet a horse that was unable to complete this lesson. I have, unfortunately, made the mistake of thinking that it would be easy. This lesson can take time and be frustrating, and if you get to a point where you're getting frustrated, switch to something else, like turning from the other side or reviewing backing, because if you're getting frustrated, so is your horse. Take a break, and then try again. When I get frustrated, I find I pay less attention to details—like *safety*. Because this exercise requires you to stand more to the side of the horse, you're at greater risk of injury when your horse gets frustrated. Remember, *safety first*, so take your time and set small goals for both you and your horse with this exercise.

My riding instructors always told me that you can't cue a horse to turn by using its shoulders, but it has always felt natural to me to use the front end to turn the horse, as well as using more conventional techniques. I've also found it to be important when riding at fast speeds or bareback. What most people don't realize is that it comes naturally when riding. However, before you get on the horse's back, you'll need to get it used to the idea from the ground.

Let's say that I want the horse's front to turn left:

1. Standing at the right shoulder, I place my left hand behind the horse's elbow. My other hand usually rests at the top of the horse's neck or against the back of the jaw.

2. To start the turn, I apply pressure with my left hand. As I apply pressure, I move my hand forward. The focus is to pressure the horse to move its leg up and forward.

3. If the horse doesn't move, I continue to

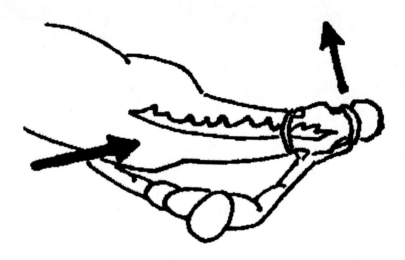

apply pressure with my left hand while I use my right to push the head and neck away.

4. Once the horse takes a step, I relax all the cues and bring my hands back to the starting position.

Focus on getting the leg on the outside of the turn to move up and in front of the inside leg. You may find that you'll need to almost grab the elbow and pull it forward the first few times to achieve this, but soon the horse will move correctly with just pressure at the shoulder.

In the end, the goal is a balanced turn, which occurs when both the front and hind ends are turning at the same time. In riding, the two cues will come very naturally. A balanced turn is smoother, quicker, and safer when working the horse in a series of turns. It doesn't look fancy, and it's not the type of thing that you'll see in the show ring. However, it's more practical and useful for the average trail or work horse.

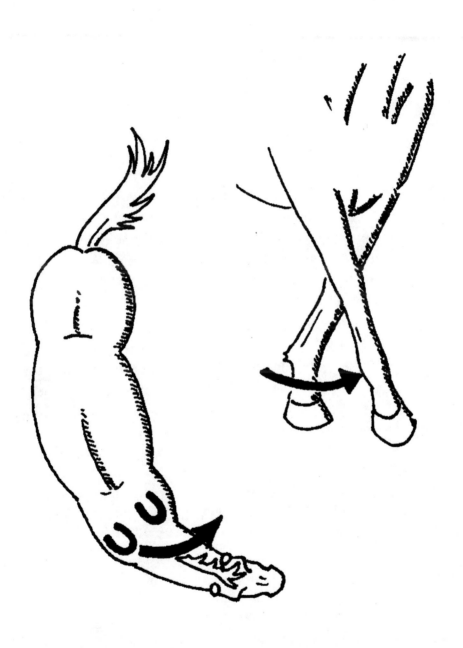

1 1

PICKING UP THE FEET

Now that the horse can lead, back up, and turn, you're ready to teach it how to pick up its feet. Lifting the feet is a difficult lesson for any horse to learn. Its biggest defenses are to either run or kick, and when you pick up a foot, you've taken away both of those options. For that reason, this can be stressful for the horse.

This is also a lesson with many different variations. Some people use a lunge whip and tap the horse until it picks up its foot. This method looks nice, but results in a horse that picks up its feet every time you touch it, and anyone who has ever wrapped a horse's leg knows what a pain that can be. Some people try rubbing the legs until they can pick them up with their hands. This method is dangerous because it puts you too close if the horse kicks.

As I said earlier, this is a hard lesson for the horse—no matter what method you use. Often a horse seems to be okay with the idea of having its legs rubbed, but will kick out once the foot is raised. I don't want to be holding that foot if the horse decides to kick with that leg. *Always think safety!*

For safety and practicality, I teach this lesson using a rope. By lifting the legs with a rope, I can keep my distance while controlling the foot and the duration it stays lifted. I can also let the horse put its foot down if it gets nervous. I prefer to use a large cotton rope about twenty feet long. This gives me plenty of rope to work with and if the horse kicks while the foot is raised, a soft rope lowers the possibility of rope burn.

Before and during this exercise, I rub the horse down with the flag—especially on the legs. I pay particular attention to the fetlock area, since this is where the rope will fall. Once the leg is raised, I rub the horse down a little. It's one thing to get the horse to pick up its leg, but it's something entirely different to get the horse to pick up a leg and get touched on the belly (or anywhere else) at the same time. A lot of horses will pick up their leg but don't like having their upper leg touched at that time. If you're going to work on your horse's feet in the future, it will have to get used to being touched anywhere while its leg is up.

I begin with the front legs.

1. Holding the lead line, I make a large loop on the ground. Depending on the horse, I either make the loop in front or behind the foot I wish to lift.

2. Then I ask the horse to move forward or backward until the foot is in the center of the loop.

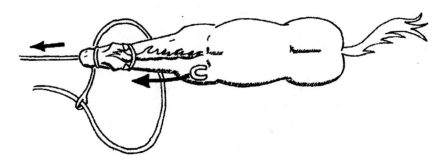

3. Next, I slowly pull the rope up around the fetlock, being prepared for the horse to move around a little. If it runs, I let it, keeping a hand on the lead line. If I have to, I let it run with the rope on its foot, trying to keep the foot rope in my hand and away from anything it might snag on.

4. If the horse is calm, I pull the rope forward, which should raise the leg off the ground. If the leg is difficult to lift, I step toward the opposite side of the horse and pull the head toward me, which helps take the weight off the leg I want to lift.

5. Next, I raise the foot out in front of the horse, just above the ground and then let it down.

6. As the horse gets accustomed to its leg being raised, I take the flag and rub the leg and body down.

7. As the leg is lifted, I rub down the leg with a saddle rope or my hand. Since both of my hands are full, I usually loop the lead line through my belt to give me a free hand.

8. While the leg is lifted, I reach down and hold the leg up with my hand, and then allow the horse to put its foot down.

9. While holding the rope for safety, I rub my hand down the leg and squeeze the fetlock at the same area where the rope is touching and lift the leg. I use the rope to help lift the leg up, if necessary.

10. With the hoof up, I gradually start swinging the foot from the front to the back, seeking to get the leg in the same position the farrier will most likely use.

11. Once I can pick up the leg with my hands, I rub the hoof, taking it in the palm of my hand and tapping on the bottom. I start with small motions and progress until I can pick up the foot and move it all around. The moving and tapping is important, because the farrier will eventually need to file the hooves and pound on them to replace the horse's shoes.

I usually stop for the day at this point. Once the horse can pick up both front legs, I let it relax for the day. For the next few training sessions, I focus only on the front legs. I like to get a horse to the point where I can hold its legs up without a rope and rub the horse down thoroughly. I take a few days doing this, to ensure that the lessons with the hind legs go smoother. I like to think that the horse will figure out that if it's okay for me to pick up its front legs, the hind legs shouldn't be any different.

The hind legs follow almost all the same rules as the front legs.

1. To begin, I place a loop around the front leg above the knee.

2. Then I twist the rope to form a large loop on the ground next to the hind foot that I want to lift.

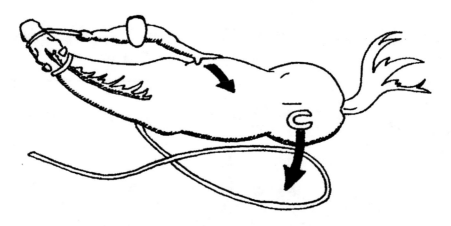

3. I apply pressure with my hand, to get the horse to move its hind end. Once it sets the foot inside the loop, I stop.

4. Standing in front of the horse's shoulder, I then take the slack out of the rope until the rope rest on the fetlock. As with the front legs, I'm ready for the horse to move or kick.

5. I make sure that there's a twist in the rope in front of the hoof I'm lifting, which acts as a safety device to keep the horse from lifting its foot out of the rope and kicking.

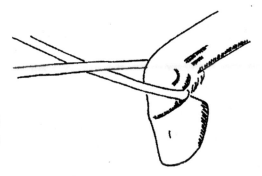

6. I pull the foot forward until the hoof clears the ground, and then let the foot down, going through the same sequence of lifting and lowering that I used with the front legs.

7. Then I lift the foot and rub the horse down thoroughly.

When I can get the horse to this point, I stop for the day. I take an extra day or two working at this level, to make sure the horse understands what's going on. I don't rush into getting my head down near the hind feet, and the rope allows me to do this with relative safety. I don't take any chances unless I have to. Remember, *think safety*—for you *and* your horse.

Once you're ready to lift the hind legs with your hands:

1. Follow the same gradual steps as before to get the horse to pick up its leg using the rope.

2. As you transition to picking up the foot with just your hands, keep the rope on the fetlock. This will help to keep the foot under control, in case the horse kicks. You won't be able to keep the horse from kicking, but you should be able to slow the kick down so you can get out of the way.

3. Once the foot can be lifted to the front by hand and the leg can be rubbed down, begin to swing the foot back to the position in

which you would pick up the foot. I usually work in stages, first swinging the foot back halfway, then all the way.

4. Once the foot is back all the way, rub down the leg, from the hock down. Pay attention to the inside of the leg and hock, as well.

5. With the leg back, again tap and rub the hoof.

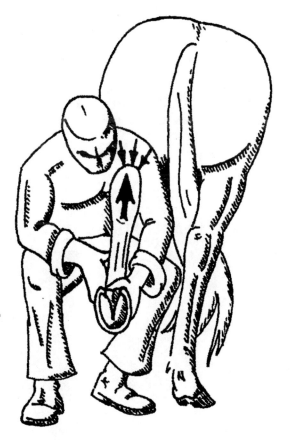

6. As the horse becomes more open to the idea, swing the leg back and rest it on your thigh, as you would to pick out the hoof. I like to bring my arm over the back of the hock and put the hock in my armpit. If the horse is going to try to kick, it'll try to lift

its leg up and off my thigh, but if the hock is in my armpit, I can control that motion long enough to get out of the way.

Again, I like to break the hind legs into two or more sessions. I've done it in one session, starting with the front end and ending with picking out the hind feet, but that can be tiring and frustrating for both you and your horse. As with anything involving a horse, the more tired and frustrated you are, the more dangerous the activity becomes. When you're dealing with an animal that can put a thousand pounds behind its kick, it pays to *go slow*. It'll take longer, but it'll be much safer.

2

Getting Saddled

12

THE BLANKET

Getting the saddle on a horse is easier if the horse is okay with the idea of having something on its back. For that reason, it's best to start with a saddle *blanket*. To the horse, the blanket is just a larger version of the flag you used earlier. Unlike the saddle, the blanket can be draped across the back with almost no chance of injury to the horse if it gets upset. Using the blanket is an easy way to progress toward putting the saddle on the horse's back.

Introduce the blanket the same way you introduced all new things to this point. Let the horse *see* the blanket, *smell* the blanket, and then *touch* the blanket. Then rub down the horse's face, neck, back, and legs with it, to get the horse used to being touched all over and seeing the blanket move around it.

The next step is to get the blanket on the horse.

1. While rubbing the horse with the blanket, rub the blanket up over the top of the neck.

2. Allow the blanket to rest there for a moment and then slide it off.

3. Rub the horse again and get the blanket over the horse's neck. Then back away a few steps, watch the horse's reaction, and then step back in and remove the blanket.

4. Eventually, you'll get to the point where the blanket can rest on the horse's neck while you ask it to take a few steps in each direction. Starting at the neck puts you at a safe point at the front of the horse's shoulder.

5. Put the blanket on the horse's neck and slide it into position on the back. Each time, give the horse a few moments with the blanket on its back. Each time you remove the blanket, give the horse a good rub to congratulate it.

6. Gradually get the horse to take a few steps in each direction. Backward seems to cause the most difficulty, because the horse needs to arch its back slightly to move backward.

If the horse gets upset at any point, let it get upset. The blanket is nice because, at this point, it can just fall off.

As you progress with the blanket, be practical. You aren't always going to drape it over the neck and slide it into position. There will be times when you'll be in a rush. At those times, you'll just throw the blanket on the horse's back, so practice that *now*. Stand at the horse's shoulder and swing the blanket upward toward the back. As the horse warms to the idea, swing the blanket up onto its back. Do this from both sides until the horse feels comfortable with your putting the blanket on its back.

13

CINCH PRESSURE

The next step is to get the horse accustomed to cinch pressure. To begin, you should be able to rub the horse thoroughly in the cinch areas. Then you can move on to applying pressure around the whole cinch area at once. This can sometimes be difficult for the horse to understand. For that reason, I like to use something that allows me the ability to get out of danger quickly—so once again, I use a rope, but a long lead line will also work well.

1. Begin by rubbing the horse with the rope.

2. Then drape the rope over the horse's back so that one end hangs down below the stomach.

3. Cautiously reach down and grab the end of the rope that's on the other side of the horse. I sometimes use an old wire coat

hanger that I've stretched out, which keeps me from having to reach under the horse.

4. Slowly raise the rope so that it lightly touches the belly.

5. Once the horse is calm about the rope touching it, tighten the rope by squeezing the ends together. If the horse gets nervous or upset, let go of the rope.

6. When you can hold the rope tightly around the horse's chest, move the rope. While it's tight, slide the rope up and down, because if your saddle shifts slightly in the future, you'll want the horse to be comfortable with that type of movement.

This exercise generally goes quickly. It's not the last thing you'll do before you put on the saddle, but it's an important middle step. It's easier to move in small, gradual steps with horse training than trying to force a horse to take large steps all at once.

THE SURCINGLE

As we progress toward putting a saddle on the horse's back, I like to take one more small step. At this point, we know the horse can accept the blanket being on its back while it moves. We also know the horse can remain calm while the cinch hugs its chest. What we *don't* know is if it will let us do *both* at the same time. We also don't know if it can handle both at an extensive walk or a trot, so the next logical thing to do is to give it a try.

Before I attempt to put a heavy saddle on a horse's back, I like to work with something a little lighter. The equipment is simple: a surcingle (made out of a piece of rope or store-bought), two stirrups that can be attached easily to the surcingle, a rope (to be tied across the chest to hold the surcingle in place), and a blanket. I use a two-inch nylon web belt (which I made) to act as a surcingle, two used stirrups, and an old blanket. This equipment was an inexpensive investment that has helped prevent injury to both my horses and myself.

1. The first step is putting the blanket on.

2. The surcingle comes next. Try to get the surcingle as tight as possible to keep the blanket in place.

3. To make sure the surcingle doesn't move backward while the horse runs, tie a rope across the chest to hold the surcingle in place.

4. Lunge the horse. Get it to walk and trot in both directions. Keep a close watch on the blanket and adjust it when necessary.

5. After the horse is used to running with the blanket and surcingle on, tie the stirrups to the surcingle.

6. Lunge the horse again, paying attention to how the horse reacts every time the stirrups bump its sides. The idea is to get the horse used to things bumping into its elbows and ribs. Your first ride is *not* the time to introduce those types of stimuli.

This exercise is a great step toward saddling. It simulates everything except the rigidity and weight of a real saddle. Yet if the horse doesn't adjust to the exercise as planned, the equipment comes off quickly, with little danger to the horse. Even if the horse really bucks and rolls, there's little possibility that the equipment will cause injury to anyone involved.

15

THE SADDLE

Before you get ready to put the saddle on the horse, make sure your equipment is ready. Whether you'll be riding English or Western, there are three questions you should ask yourself before you begin.

1. What kind of shape is my saddle in?

If you're going to use an older saddle, check to make sure everything is in good working condition. Make sure the padding is intact on the bottom of the saddle. Sometimes, on older saddles, nails have worked free from the saddle tree and can poke through the padding. Make sure the saddle tree is solid. If the tree is broken, the saddle will distribute pressure incorrectly on the horse's back, causing pain. Check all the rigging. Are the cinch straps intact and free of rot or breaks? Ten minutes of inspection can save you and your horse a lot of pain and money.

2. Is your saddle too heavy?

The horse will handle the weight of whatever saddle you put on it. What you need to ask yourself is, can I handle the weight? I often see people get to this part of the training and wonder why the horse is having such a hard time. They don't realize that the horse gets a little nervous as the rider grunts, strains, and makes all sorts of weird movements trying to get a heavy saddle on its back. A good rule of thumb is: if you can't hold the saddle in one arm, it's probably too heavy. New saddles are usually made of synthetics, which make them lighter. They might not be as macho, but they're a great alternative to heavy leather saddles. Try to stay away from those old, worn-out, back-buster saddles hiding in everyone's barn. They were usually set aside for a reason, and are more suited to be decorations than working tools.

3. What equipment do I need?

Obviously, you'll need a saddle, but what kind? The horn and the deep seat have convinced me to make Western my saddle of choice for breaking wild horses. Half of the time, the first ride is easy. The other half—well, the other half is where the term *breaking* comes from. All of the groundwork you've done limits your chances of a rough ride, but the possibility remains, so make sure you have the right stuff. A good saddle and strong cinches are a necessity. I use a regular heart girth cinch, a hind cinch, and a chest strap. The chest strap keeps the saddle from moving back too far, and the hind cinch keeps the saddle from bouncing too much. No matter what saddle you use, use a chest strap and hind cinch whenever possible.

Another piece of equipment that I've learned to love is a *blanket loop*. A blanket loop is a small piece of leather tied to the blanket and then tied again to the saddle horn. This loop helps keep the blanket from moving backward. It may seem like an insignificant detail, but if the blanket moves backward, it can fall out from under the saddle. If the blanket falls free, the saddle will suddenly be loose on the horse, and can shift forward or backward. If you aren't using a chest strap, the saddle can even rotate so that the seat is *under* the horse. This rotation presents a dangerous situation for the horse, and for the unfortunate rider who may still be in the seat. It may seem like a small, unimportant piece of equipment, but since I've been using it, I've never had to dismount and adjust a saddle blanket.

PUTTING ON THE SADDLE

Before you get ready to put the saddle on, bring it into view of the horse. I usually set it on the fence at about the height it will be on the horse. Then I lunge the horse so that it runs by the saddle. At first, the horse will try to stay clear of it, but, eventually, the horse calms down. Then I bring the horse up to smell the saddle. Once the horse has smelled it, I take it off the fence and bring it toward the horse. I usually have to stop and let the horse smell it again while it's in my hands. Once the horse is used to seeing the saddle, I start going through the motions of putting it on.

1. While standing at the shoulder of the horse, I raise the saddle up and let it touch the side of the horse's body—usually on the shoulder.

2. Next I put the saddle on the horse's back. At first, the saddle is far forward, almost on the neck. This is safer, because I can put it up on the horse's back while I'm standing by the shoulder, out of reach of the hind legs.

3. Once the saddle is on the horse, I slide it back into place, and then, almost immediately, take it off the horse.

4. After doing this a few times, I start leaving the saddle on for longer periods. In essence, I'm repeating the blanket exercise, using the saddle instead.

Having a saddle attached for the first time can be a bit touchy for any horse. However, slow movements, and some thinking ahead, will help keep you out of trouble.

1. Put all your rigging (cinch straps, chest straps, etc.) up over the saddle seat.

2. Put the stirrup that will be on the far side of the horse over the saddle or on the saddle horn.

3. Put the saddle pad on the horse's back. Put it a little forward of where it should be under the saddle. At first, I put it about halfway down the neck.

4. Place the saddle gently on the saddle pad and slide both the saddle and pad back into place. This will ensure that the horse has all its hair going in the right direction, since the horse's comfort will have a big impact on your riding experience.

5. Walk to the other side of the horse. Stand at the shoulder and let the stirrup down, but don't let it flop. Eventually, your horse will learn it's okay, but for now, letting the stirrup flop down against the horse is a dangerous thing to do.

6. Lift the chest strap off the seat of the saddle.

7. Lift the chest and hind cinch off the seat of the saddle. Be careful, because sometimes the buckles on the cinches can get caught up on the saddle and move it just enough to make the horse nervous.

8. Take the chest strap across the chest to the other side of the saddle and buckle the chest strap into place. At this point, if the horse goes nuts for some reason, the saddle will fall off in front of the horse. If it

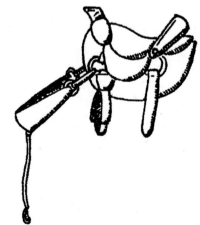

falls to the front of the horse, there's little that can happen that will hurt either the horse or your saddle.

9. Attach the chest cinch (girth), but don't tighten it all the way yet. Just get it snug. If the horse goes crazy, the saddle might slip to the side slightly, but it shouldn't end up under the horse or in front of it.

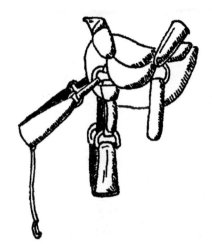

10. Attach the hind cinch. It should be snug. A loose cinch strap (one that you can fit a closed fist through) serves no purpose. A snug hind cinch (one that allows you to pass a flat hand through easily) keeps the back of the saddle from bouncing, but is loose enough not to agitate the horse.

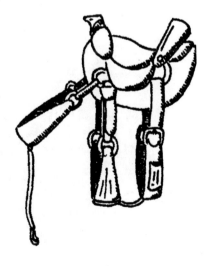

11. Attach the chest strap to the chest cinch (girth) between the front legs.

12. From under the pummel or under the saddle horn, pull the saddle blanket up and tie it into place. This will form a little tent in the blanket at the base of the neck. That little tent will afford the horse more comfort to move its neck, and securing the blanket in place will keep it from slipping free of the saddle.

13. Tighten the chest cinch (girth). The girth should be tight enough to allow only a few fingers to slide under it.

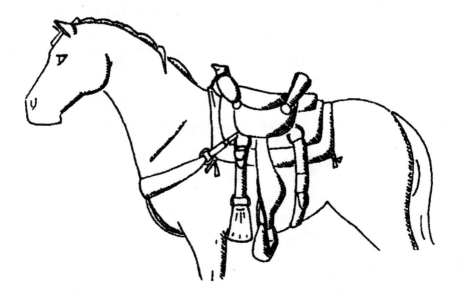

Now that the horse is saddled correctly, lunge it in both directions until it settles into a relaxed gait. Move the horse forward and backward. At this point, try to refrain from getting in close to do turns. Just let the horse get accustomed to the feel and sound of the saddle.

GETTING USED TO THE SADDLE

Once the horse is comfortable lunging with the saddle on, you'll want to move in closer. From this point on, anything you do toward getting on the horse's back will require you to touch the saddle in some way. For example, you'll probably need to hold the stirrup while you put your foot in position to mount, or you'll apply pressure on the saddle as you pull yourself up into the seat. No matter how you mount, you'll be touching and moving the saddle while it's on the horse's back. To get the horse accustomed to this, there are a few things you'll want to do while the saddle is on.

1. Go through the flagging exercises with the horse while the saddle is on.

2. Rub the horse down with a saddle rope. The saddle rope will make different sounds against a hard leather saddle, so be prepared for any type of reaction.

3. Pull and push on the saddle horn. Although it's better for the horse's back if you don't use the saddle horn to support yourself as you mount, there are times when it can't be avoided, so get the horse to accept you moving the saddle in that way.

4. Move the stirrups. Gradually lift and lower them until you can place the stirrup over the saddle horn. If you're the type who just drops the stirrups when you're saddling, now's the time to introduce that idea. Gently lift and release the stirrup so it drops to the horse's side, but be ready for the horse to jump forward the first few times. It's also good to pull and "snap" the stirrups, which will help get the horse used to having you adjust the stirrup length. You don't actually need to adjust the length to do this. Just sharply pull down on the stirrup to make the leather snap.

One of the most frightening things for the horse is the feeling of something moving on its back for the first time, and your first ride isn't the best time to introduce that feeling. No one's first ride is perfect, and you'll have to shift your weight a lot. You can get the horse to be aware of that feeling from the ground by attaching a rope around the saddle, around the horn, around the seat, or through the pummel of an English saddle—all are good options.

While the horse lunges in a circle, pull the rope that's attached to the saddle. This will simulate your shifting weight as the horse moves. Don't make the pulling motion constant. Pull, judge the horse's reaction, relax the saddle rope, and then pull the rope again. Try some strong pulls on the saddle and some softer, more rapid pulls. Make sure to do this with the horse moving in both directions.

The main focus to this exercise is to watch the horse's reaction. It's best to keep the horse working at a trot. As you pull on the saddle, the horse will initially jump, stumble slightly, or rapidly pick up the pace for a few strides. You want to progress to a point where the horse doesn't break its gait. You want the horse to become accustomed to the possibility that the saddle may move slightly. In the beginning, even very little saddle movement may be a complete surprise to the horse.

GETTING ON FROM THE FENCE

One of the most nerve-racking things you'll ever do with your horse is that first ride. No matter how many horses you end up training and no matter how many precautions you take, your heart will beat a little faster every time. Don't be ashamed, the horse's heart is beating just as fast. That's why building up *slowly* to this point is so important. Anything you can do before this moment will have helped build your confidence and your horse's acceptance of the idea.

One of the hardest things for the horse to get over is the idea of you being above and behind it. If the horse still thinks of you as predator, it will be hard for the horse to allow you in that position. Use a fence to get the horse to accept your being above and behind it. A tall, sturdy fence is a great training tool. I built my round pen with high fences (about six feet tall) so I could use them for this part of the training. When I'm holding the top rail of the fence, my hips are just about at the same height they'd be if I were in the saddle. From the fence, I can put weight in the saddle, just as if I were riding, while holding on to the fence for a quick escape.

It sometimes takes a little time to get the horse comfortable with walking along the fence. You can do this by lunging the horse near the fence. Gradually get the horse going in a smaller circle until it's walking between you and the fence with only a few feet to spare. Once it can do that, I like to lead the horse along the fence.

Periodically, I stop and climb up a few rails. Sometimes I climb up and then turn and rub the horse while I'm only slightly up on the fence. Eventually, the horse should be okay with you climbing up the fence next to it while it stands still. This will also come in handy if you have trouble mounting from the ground and need to climb up on something in order to get on the horse.

At this point, you want to rub the horse down. By now, you should know what steps your horse needs to get it calm. Gradually work through those steps so that you can get back behind the horse's shoulders. You should be able to rub it down thoroughly with the saddle rope, your hands, your feet, your legs, and any other training aid you feel could be of benefit. If the horse is wearing the saddle, shake the saddle. Jerk the stirrups. Carefully reach over the saddle and get the other stirrup to move. Do whatever you can to get your horse comfortable with you being on the fence, and with your touching it from that position. Just *don't* let go of the fence.

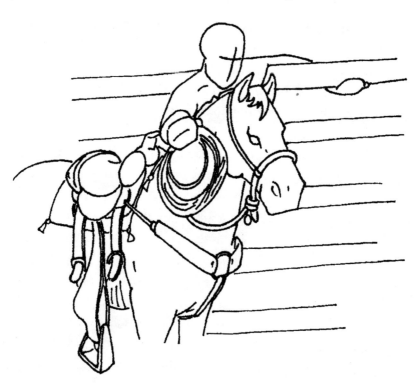

With this lesson, I like to get to a point where I can sit in the saddle while securely holding on to the fence. For this, I start with one knee in the seat of the saddle. I gradually get to a point where I can extend my leg over to the other side of the saddle—without putting my butt in the seat. Once the horse is okay with that, I begin to sit in the saddle so it can feel what the majority of my weight feels like. The most important thing to keep in mind is to *not* put your feet in the stirrups until you're ready to ride! Once your feet are in the stirrups, you risk having them caught up in the stirrups and yanking you from the fence. As long as you keep your feet out of the stirrups and you keep a firm grip on the fence, you can pull yourself off the horse if it gets scared and runs. You might fall off the fence after the horse runs away, but that's nicer than falling off a running, bucking horse!

Once you've gotten this far, you'll realize that you could start your first ride from this point, but there are two big differences. You'll need to get your feet in the stirrups and you'll have to let go of the fence. As far as the stirrups go, I recommend going slowly and making sure you can do it without using your hands. In other words, make sure you can find the stirrups with your foot. It's a good idea to wet your stirrups down while the saddle is on the saddle rack and then use a piece of wood to twist both stirrups into position. When the leather dries, you'll find the stirrups will stay twisted in position, making it easier to get your foot into the stirrups. The last thing you want at this point is to be kicking your horse in the side while looking for a stirrup.

The fence method of mounting for the first few rides is great. I use it a lot. It makes it easier to mount tall horses for the first time, it eliminates the awkwardness of standing on one leg while the other is up in the stirrup, and most importantly, it narrows the options for the horse. When mounting from the fence, you know there are only two directions the horse can go—to the side or forward. That may not seem like much help, but if the horse does run or buck, most people will fall off with the first movement. The horse catches them off-guard because they didn't know which way the horse would go. If you can get past that first jolt forward or that first quick twist to the side, your odds of staying on through the rest will be much better. I'll discuss how to get the horse to move away from the fence in greater detail later, but for now, just keep in mind that your first ride can start right from the fence.

MOUNTING FROM
THE GROUND

If you don't have a tall enough fence or if the fence mount just isn't for you, you can mount from the ground. Before I begin, put any idea of using a mounting block out of your mind. A mounting block is great—once you know the horse is good about mounting. However, until the horse will *let* you mount it, a mounting block can be dangerous. Mounting blocks can fall over. The horse, once you get on, can trip and fall on the mounting block, hurting the horse and, more importantly, *you*. I've seen people get one foot in the stirrup and then have the horse pull them off the mounting block and across the arena in an unpleasant manner.

Most notably, a mounting block puts you just at the right place to get kicked to the other side of the yard. It's like tee ball, when you place a ball on a stand so a small child can hit it more easily with a bat. Just like tee ball, mounting blocks are great to use once the horse understands that you're going to ride. They are great for the horse, because they put less stress on a horse's back. However, when it comes to the first few rides, they present more of a danger than they're worth.

To begin mounting from the ground, you want to be standing at the shoulder of the horse, facing its hind end. It may seem as if you're more forward than you're used to, but it keeps you out of the range of the hind feet. Take a hold of the saddle horn and lean while pulling down. Sometimes I put one hand on the saddle horn and one in the stirrup, so I can really put some weight down, as if I were stepping up. Do this on both sides. Remember, you eventually should be able to mount from either side of the horse. Now is also a good time to check the tightness of the chest cinch (girth). The saddle should shift only slightly as you lean and apply pressure.

Once you can lean on the saddle, you'll want to start lifting a foot into the stirrup. Once again, you want to stand at the horse's shoulder, looking toward the hind end. With the hand that is closest to the horse, take ahold of the horse at the back of its neck. Use your other hand to steady the stirrup as you lift your leg up, and then use it to steady the saddle. When you're stepping into the stirrup, there are two important ideas to keep in mind.

1. Only the ball of your foot should be in the stirrup. If you put your foot in any further, you risk getting your foot wedged in the stirrup. The heels on your boots shouldn't be touching the stirrup. Many people make that mistake and get hurt because they couldn't get their feet clear of the stirrup in an emergency.

2. Keep your raised leg against the horse's shoulder. This is where many people make a mistake. As they mount, they begin with their knee against the horse or they turn toward the horse on the way up, causing them to dig their knee into the horse's side as they lift themselves into the saddle. A well-broke horse won't care if you bump it in the side with your knee, but a horse that hasn't been ridden yet will care! Placing your leg against

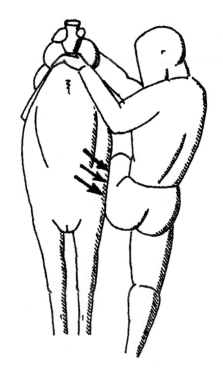

the shoulder and raising yourself up while you're facing the hind end of the horse is no more difficult. Once you get to a point where you're standing in the stirrup with your leg fully extended, then you can turn in, toward the horse.

When you're ready to actually step up into the saddle, you need to start paying close attention to the horse. Once you start standing up in the saddle, you've got nothing but the horse to hold on to. If the horse does anything at that point, there are only two things you can do. You can either hold on and hope for the best or get yourself clear and start again. I advise getting yourself clear.

It's at this point that putting only the ball of your foot in the stirrup is most important. If the horse decides to start bucking while you're in the process of getting on, you want to be able to push yourself away from the horse easily. When your feet (or your butt) reach the ground—move away quickly. Before I start stepping up into the saddle, I like to take a few seconds and go over what I'll do if something goes wrong. From this point, always be acutely aware of everything that's going on.

With one hand on the saddle, and one foot in the stirrup, step up. Remain facing the hind end of the horse as you raise yourself. You may find that you'll need to raise yourself up in stages to keep your horse calm. It's also beneficial to switch to the other side of the horse and try it from that side. Doing that will give you a reliable horse that can be mounted from either side. Continue lifting yourself up until you can stand in the stirrup from both sides of the horse.

Once you can stand in the stirrup, you can start getting the horse used to your being up there. Just like with the fence, gradually start rubbing down the opposite side of the horse. I usually start by reaching over and rubbing the neck and shoulders. Then I move on to shifting the other stirrup.

Gradually, start putting your knee in the saddle seat. Do whatever you feel necessary to make the horse more comfortable and yourself more confident. The horse might move, so don't lean too far over the saddle, because if you lean too far and the horse moves, you may end up falling over the other side onto your head.

When I finally put my other leg over, I usually dismount quickly. I do that a couple of times if I can, without putting my foot in the other stirrup. I like to get the horse used to me just sitting on its back first.

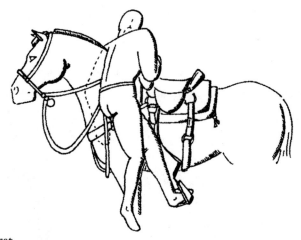

When I'm ready to get the horse moving, I'll get my foot in the stirrup. Just like before, it works best if you don't have to kick your foot around, looking for the stirrup. If you have to, carefully reach down and use your hand to steady the stirrup. If you have to do that, always keep your weight over the center of the horse. Don't lean out to the side to see what you're doing. Be ready to ride. If the horse is okay with you just sitting still, you'll have a few seconds to get ready for the next big step.

3

Riding

20

THE ADVANTAGES
OF BAREBACK

There are many ways to ride a horse, but after years of riding, I've personally found that bareback is the best way. I'm not just saying that because I don't like taking the time to tack up a horse before I ride. Bareback riding is the best way to teach a horse to respond to leg cues and it's a great way to teach a horse the basics and any other riding exercise—including jumping. Bareback riding is also the best way to teach riders how to keep a good grip on the horse and to use their legs and weight to keep them balanced on the horse's back. It forces riders to learn to ride instinctively without falling off.

Bareback riding isn't popular. Don't get me wrong, people like to sit bareback on a horse and walk around, maybe even trot. But few people like to really *ride* bareback, with the horse running all out and the wind blowing in their faces.

Bareback riding is more difficult than riding with a saddle because you have to use your legs more and you need to maintain a good posture just to stay on the horse. You may find yourself hitting the ground more—at first—but riding without a saddle will improve your riding skills more than anything else. Many people seem dependent on the stirrups of the saddle, but anything you can do with stirrups, you can do without them, as well. A good bareback rider can run a horse, jump a horse, and can even cut cows or do dressage.

The most important benefit to bareback riding is what happens when you put a bareback rider back into a saddle. A good bareback rider is even better in a saddle. They have more balance and control, and they aren't going to come out of the saddle until they're ready to come out. Of all riding lessons, learning how to stay on, no matter what, is the hardest. With bareback riding, you'll learn to use your legs and weight to stay on, and most significantly, you'll learn when and how to fall off. No matter what you might think about bareback riding, it's at the very least a great tool to increase your riding potential.

I prefer to do everything bareback. I do use a saddle for the first few rides and then intermittently, just to keep the horse familiar with it, but bareback riding is what I love. Bareback riding has increased my riding ability much more than any other factor, and continues to increase my abilities.

I also like the way it allows me to communicate with my horses. I can teach them to respond to even the lightest leg cue, and I can also feel them under me. It may sound weird, but I can even feel their heartbeat. I can feel how their backs move as they run, and I feel more in tune with my horses when I keep a saddle off them.

When I do put the saddle on, I notice a huge difference—not in the way *they* respond, but in the way I *ride*. Bareback riding makes me feel more secure in the saddle, and more in control than I ever felt before I started riding bareback. So for me, bareback riding will always be the way I prefer to ride and teach a horse.

Because I think bareback riding is so important and beneficial and because I think most people don't know how to ride without a saddle, the lessons in this book are designed to encourage *you* to ride bareback, too. You can do it all with a saddle (and for the first few rides, I recommend that you do), but both you and your horse will be missing out on something special.

If it's not physically possible for you to ride bareback, then use a saddle. However, if you can withstand some muscle pain and a few bumps and bruises, give bareback riding a try. The benefits outweigh any pain you'll suffer. After all, sore muscles will go away.

Stirrups are like training wheels on bicycles. They serve a purpose and make us feel safer. However, to really experience a great bike ride, the training wheels need to come off. Stick to it, and I guarantee that after riding bareback, you'll see a genuine improvement in your riding.

21

RIDING POSTURE

With any style of riding, posture is one of the most important aspects. In fact, posture is so important in riding that it's often the difference between staying on a horse and falling off. There's little difference between the posture used in bareback riding and the posture used in any other sort of riding. For a person with poor posture in the saddle, bareback riding can be a valuable tool for improving a less-than-desirable riding posture. It's easier to describe good riding posture by comparing it to poor riding posture.

1. **Find your center.** When looking at a centered rider, the horse's head and the rider's head should be in line. The rider's shoulders should be parallel to the horizon, as should the hands. The hands should be spaced equally from the horse on both sides. The rider's knees should also be at the same height. Having a centered posture allows you to apply pressure equally to both sides of the horse. An off-center rider leans to one side of the horse, which is the result of poor head placement. If the rider's head is tilted to the side, the shoulders will tilt, and if the shoulders tilt, the hands won't be even. Uneven shoulders will also cause the knees to be uneven. If the rider is leaning toward one side, they'll always be putting more pressure on that side of the horse. Off-center riding also puts the rider at a greater risk of falling during turns, as well as causing problems cueing the horse to turn and increase speed.

2. **Proper leg position.** Proper leg position helps you grip the horse and communicate with it. There's a groove that is created behind the horse's shoulder and in front of the rib cage, and a rider's leg fits perfectly into that groove. When the leg is in that groove, the rider's thigh is parallel to the horse's shoulder blade. The knee points straight forward and the lower leg will bend back slightly, so the rider's feet fall just behind the horse's elbow. This leg position will allow you to use the horse's shoulders to post slightly while riding at a trot. It will also help you use the rib cage as a means to stay forward on the horse's back, which comes in handy when you start to increase speed or when you're running up a hill.

   Good leg position will help you keep a grip on the horse, while poor leg position invites danger. It's usually the knees that cause poor leg position. If you allow your knees to turn out, you'll cause your thighs to come away from the horse and your lower legs to dangle. Turning your knees out puts all the gripping pressure on the back of your legs and butt. It will cause your hips to come up off the horse's back, which will make it difficult to keep a comfortable seat. Overall, poor leg position will decrease the amount of contact your body makes with the horse's body. The parts of your body that do contact the horse are the weaker parts of your legs, which decreases the amount of grip you'll get on the horse and increases the likelihood of a fall.

3. **Proper foot position.** Stirrups are like training wheels. They make us feel safe, but they can also impede our progress. Without stirrups, the feet should be relaxed. Let your feet hang down freely, with no tension. With your feet relaxed, you'll be able to use your legs to grip more easily. If you concentrate on pointing your heels down, you create tension in the back of your legs. The back of your legs shouldn't be touching the horse, and the parts that do touch the horse won't be able to relax and contract if the back of your leg is tensed. Even if you use stirrups, don't put the pressure in your heels. Though your heels should be lower, the pressure should all be in the ball of the foot, with your ankle remaining relaxed. With the pressure in the ball of the foot, you'll be able to move your legs in reaction to the horse's movements. You can post more easily, adjust to turns, and stop and run more easily. By keeping the heel and ankle relaxed, you'll keep your whole leg relaxed and ready.

4. **Head up.** When you learned to drive a car, you learned to look at least two car lengths ahead. When you're driving a horse, you should be looking two horse lengths ahead. Keeping your head up will also help you keep your balance. We'll discuss that more when we talk about turns. Just keep in mind that you won't be able to see where you're going if you're constantly looking down at the horse.

With all that said, there are two more important lessons that many people never learn.

1. Riding shouldn't impede the horse's movement. All riding should be done in a way to work *with* the horse, not against it. Learn how to move in rhythm with your horse.

2. Learn to fall. The most important lesson in riding is that you're going to fall sometimes. Everyone falls. I've fallen off more times than I can remember. It just happens. The best thing to know about falling is *to try not to fight it.* People who try to hold on when they're already halfway to the ground get hurt. People who let go walk away with the fewest injuries. If your horse starts bucking or doing something crazy and you don't know if you can hold on, choose the right moment and *get off.* It's easier said than done, but anyone who has ever fallen off a horse knows that there's a moment when you have to make a choice—stay and fight, or fall. Almost every time I get the choice, I choose to fall. If a horse is doing something I can't handle, I choose when to let go—and I fall. When I let go, I remember to use my hands and arms to protect my head and neck. Don't put your arms out to break your fall, because arms will break. Land on your shoulder and side, if you can.

   Once you hit the ground, *run.* I once was riding a horse when I felt her start to slide. I was able to fall to the side just as she fell. When the two of us hit the ground, I made the mistake of staying on the ground while I caught my breath. The horse stood up, slipped again, and came crashing down—right onto my back. That's when I learned that when you hit the ground, it's time to start running! You're going to fall. Everyone does. Anyone who says they either haven't fallen or hardly ever fall—well, those people probably aren't trying hard enough.

22

THE FIRST TURN

One of the best ways to begin your first ride is with a turn. Turning first does a couple things for you:

1. A horse that's turning a tight circle isn't running or bucking straight forward. It may seem like a small detail, but it's one that can make a big difference.

2. A turn is easier for the horse to understand. Forward cues can be difficult for a horse at first. If someone jumped on my back and started kicking me in the kidneys, I wouldn't necessarily understand what it meant, either! Turning allows you to use your reins and legs in conjunction to tell the horse where you want to go. If you're pulling the horse's head to the side, it will eventually have to move, just to keep its balance.

As with any step in riding, there are cues that can be given to get your horse to move, but usually, you'll start by giving the least physical cue. Then, if that doesn't work, you'll progress through the various cues until the horse begins to move. Each cue gets a little more physical and a little less subtle. As time goes by, the horse will pick up on those subtle cues and your riding will become seemingly effortless.

For turns, the most, subtle cue comes from your head.

1. Turn and look where you want to go. Your body will go where your head tells it to go. If you turn your head to the left, your shoulders will turn that way. As your shoulders turn, your spine will twist and cause your hips to turn. As your shoulders and hips turn, your arms and legs move. As your head turns to the left, your left arm and leg will drop back slightly as your right arm and leg move forward—and all that movement comes from just turning to see where you want to go.

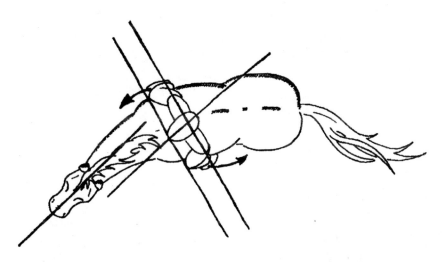

2. If that doesn't get the horse to turn, exaggerate your leg movement. Apply more pressure with the leg that's on the inside of the turn. Visualize lifting and pushing the rib cage out of the way. Let the outside leg come forward slightly to push the horse around the center of the turn. Try not to kick with either leg. Just apply pressure.

3. The last step is to use the reins. If the horse still isn't moving, exaggerate the rein movement. Gradually increase the pressure on the inside rein. (The direction you're turning.) Remember that you'll also need to relax the outside rein by moving that hand forward a little. If you *don't* relax the outside rein, the horse will turn its head to the inside of the turn and take all the slack out

of the other rein. Then the horse will feel pressure on both reins and not know what to do. Don't jerk at the reins—that's a good way to make the horse nervous. Only apply steady, constant pressure to the inside rein.

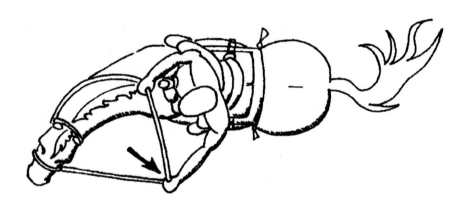

Once the horse begins to move, relax everything and congratulate the horse before asking again. By relaxing the pressure, you're telling the horse that it did the right thing. If you congratulate every slight improvement, the horse will progress more calmly and quickly. As the training goes on, you can increase what you're asking. Instead of asking for one step in the right direction, ask for two or three, and then stop and congratulate the horse. Eventually, the horse will be able to move in any direction without your constant reassurance that it's doing the right thing. Until then, praise every bit of progress as much as you can. If the horse makes a mistake, stop and try again. The horse will be less stressed, and will learn more quickly.

Eventually, you'll be able to get the horse to make a good turn just by turning your head and shifting your weight. The horse will always try to remain as balanced as possible, and shifting your weight will make the horse move in order to compensate for your shift. However, this isn't something that should be attempted at first. Leaning and shifting your weight will cause you to be off balance. If you and your horse aren't yet working together in harmony, the horse won't compensate for your lean, and you may lean your way right off your horse's back.

23

BACKING/STOPPING

The next big movement is backing/stopping. I find that horses want to do this on their own at first. In fact, when I get on a horse for the first time, it often takes a few steps back before it realizes that I'm still on—then it doesn't want to move at all.

The trick to backing/stopping is getting the horse to do it on command. As you learn how to back your horse, notice that the same steps are employed to *stop*. This is important for future steps.

Backing/stopping a horse is simple, and it can be done a number of different ways, but I'm going to describe the methods I like to use. I prefer these methods because they teach the horse to give in to pressure and to adjust to how my body is positioned.

1. Again, start with the head. Move your head back slightly, keeping your chin down. The idea is to shift your weight back. You should notice your shoulders move back a very small amount and your legs move forward. By shifting your weight back a little, your movements are going against what the horse is doing. This leaves the horse with three options: decide that you need to come off its back (so be *ready*), decide to slow down and stop so you can start working with it again, or shift its weight back so it can be balanced with you. This is a very subtle cue that your horse won't pick up right away, but in the long run, getting yourself out of balance with your horse's rhythm is the quickest way to get its

attention. Start by doing this, but don't expect your horse to understand it the first time.

2. If the horse doesn't respond, use the reins. As you lean back, even though you're only leaning back slightly, your hands will come back naturally, as well. Exaggerate that movement while applying steadily increasing pressure on the reins. As the horse begins to learn backing and stopping, I like to have something over its nose, so I use a bosal when I'm using reins. However, if you're teaching a horse to use a bit, it's also a good idea to have a halter (with a separate set of reins) on the horse. Most horses I've worked with fight the bit at first, so I use the halter and separate set of reins as a safety device. If the horse is fighting the bit and

won't stop, I can use the halter to put pressure on its face, which will make it hard for the horse to run faster.

3. If the horse still doesn't move back, alternate pressure on the reins. Always apply pressure to *both* reins, but begin to fluctuate the *amount* of pressure, putting a little more on the right rein, then the left, then the right, and so on.

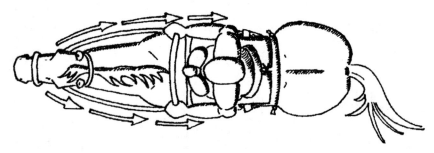

4. The last step is something for bareback riders. Exaggerate your leg cue. As I said before, when you lean backward, your legs will swing forward. Exaggerate that fact by bringing your legs up to the point of the horse's shoulders. The idea is to make it awkward for the horse to move its legs forward. That will slow it down and get it to stop. Then, if you keep applying that pressure, you'll get it to back up. Apply pressure at the shoulders, just like the ground exercise you did for backing.

If your horse still won't stop, make it turn. Remember that it's hard for it to run fast if it's turning a tight circle. Pull its head to the side to break that forward movement. The horse will either come to a stop right away or slow down significantly. A runaway horse is usually scared, and jerking back on the reins won't calm it down. In fact, very little will calm a horse down at that point, but if *you* can stay calm, you can control *where* the horse runs. Just remember, if the horse won't stop, pull it into a circle.

24

STEPPING FORWARD

Forward cues can be difficult with a fresh horse. That's why I focus on this after everything else. Most horses have no problem going forward. In fact, most horses usually like to go forward right away—at a fast speed. The difficulty lies in getting them to move forward when you want them to and at the right speed, but with courage and patience, you can do it.

When you're teaching a horse to move forward, there are three basic rules to keep in mind:

1. Try to use the easiest cues. For a forward movement, that usually means a little squeeze—not a kick. Kicking is wrong for two reasons. First, it's just not nice. (Have someone kick *you* in the kidneys and see if you like how it feels.) Second, if you're swinging your legs to kick the horse, your legs are coming away from the horse's body, and when the horse begins to move, you might not be able to hold on.

    The best thing I've found for a forward cue is a simple squeeze with the legs. If that doesn't work, you can use your heels to apply increased pressure to the rib cage. If you still can't get the horse to move forward, tap your heels lightly on the horse's sides. Just remember that your legs should never swing so much that they leave the horse's sides. If none of those things work, turn the horse, getting it to move in either direction. Then turn it into a straight forward motion. Sometimes a horse gets braced up and just needs a little side-step to get started.

2. A horse can't move forward if you're holding it back. This is one of the most frequent mistakes I see made by riders at every level. The horse can't be expected to move forward smoothly if you're holding the reins back tightly in anticipation of a lunge forward. If you want the horse to move forward, you have to be willing to take an awkward leap of faith.

3. Be prepared. If you're working with a young, untrained, horse, be ready for it to suddenly get the idea. Many people will sit on the horse's back and kick the horse in the sides until, suddenly, when the rider least expects it, the horse figures out what they're asking. At that point, the horse jumps forward—and the rider lands on the ground. Be ready for anything! Relax and stay focused. Curve your back and lean forward slightly. That will help your body absorb some of the shock if the horse jumps forward, and it'll

lower your center of gravity over the horse's center of gravity, which will help you stay balanced. Always keep your legs close to the horse's body. You grip the horse with your legs, so keep your legs tight against the horse at all times.

When the horse starts moving forward on command, don't worry too much about what speed it's going. For the first few attempts, the horse will probably start going forward quicker than you want it to, but it will eventually realize that you're not out to hurt it and that you're only asking it to walk. Every time the horse starts out too quickly, give it a moment to understand that they did the right thing by moving forward, and then pull back the reins slightly to either slow the horse into a walk or get it to stop. Continue with that start and stop technique until the horse is able to walk forward in a relatively calm matter.

25

TURNING WHILE WALKING

The next step is teaching the horse how to walk and turn without stopping. Most horses will initially want to stop every time you ask them to turn, so it will take some effort to get your horse to walk and turn without stopping. This isn't something that will be accomplished quickly. In fact, it's something you'll probably need to incorporate into many other training sessions.

One of the easiest ways to begin is by walking a figure-eight pattern. Start with as large a pattern as you can—the larger the figure-eight, the less dramatic the turns will be, and the less dramatic the turns, the easier it will be to keep the horse moving forward. Whether you use traffic cones or marks in the dirt, give yourself some focus points to turn around. It will be easier for both you and the horse if you have objects to focus on when turning.

Your goal is to ask for a turn while keeping the horse moving in a forward direction. Your turns should be as slight as possible to begin with—not nearly as dramatic as the turns we discussed earlier. The same cues are used: leg pressure, head turns, and a balance shift. The only difference is in the *rein cues.* Instead of pulling the rein out to the side to pull the horse's head toward the turn, pull straight back. A slight turn requires slight pressure on the side that you want to turn toward.

As the horse improves, change the size of the figure-eight to increase or decrease the sharpness of the turns. If possible, incorporate both sharp turns and mild turns in this exercise, to help the horse learn the difference. The more creative you are, the better your horse will get.

26

GOING FASTER

Once the horse can walk and turn without stopping, you can begin to work on getting it to move faster, and getting a horse to go faster isn't terribly complicated. In fact, you've probably already gone faster than you've wanted to go on a number of occasions! Faster is easy for horses, but getting your horse to increase speed in a controlled fashion is more difficult. The most important ideas with going faster are the same as with the walk.

1. Use the simplest forward cues possible.

2. Don't hold the horse back.

3. Be prepared to move.

For each speed, I'll discuss how those three rules apply.

The Trot

The horse can go into a trot from a standstill or a walk. The cues for both are the same, but it will be easier for both of you to start from a walk. When you're at a walk and you want the horse to trot, all you have to do is *squeeze*. I focus on applying pressure with my heels and trying to lift and push the rib cage forward. If that doesn't work, I may tap the horse's sides with my heels. Just remember, a tap is one thing—a kick is something very different.

If nothing seems to be working to get the horse to go faster, I resort to using a quirt. Made of rope or leather, a quirt is a soft, flexible tool used to drive a horse forward. Basically, a quirt is an extension of your hand that can be used to tap the horse on the hind end. That light tapping is usually all you'll need to get the horse moving—mostly because it scares the horse at first.

Eventually, the horse will understand what being tapped by the quirt means, and then you'll be able to tap it on the shoulder to get it moving. I find that I often have to teach the trot while tapping the horse on the butt, but once I'm ready to go even faster, I can just tap it on the shoulder. After a while, you won't need to use the quirt at all, but at first, it may be necessary.

No matter what cue you're trying, keep in mind that the horse can't move faster unless you let it, so fight your anxiety and relax the reins. Keep a tight hold of the reins so they won't come out of your hands, but let them relax enough to let the horse move faster. If the horse goes faster than you want, you can always pull back on the reins and ask again.

Finally, be *ready*. The horse is probably going to jump into a trot the first few times, so you'll want to relax your back and lean forward slightly to lower your center of gravity. Also be ready to go faster than you wanted to go. Every horse is capable of going from a walk to a fast run very quickly, so be ready! As you did with the walk, let the horse take a few steps forward, just to let it know that it was a good thing it moved forward faster. Then pull it back to the speed you really wanted to travel at.

The Canter

You can get a horse to canter from a walk, but try it from a trot at first. The canter is an odd pace. It's a "3 beat" movement. There are also two types of canter. There's a left canter, in which the left front foot lands first, and a right canter, in which the right front foot lands first. For now, keep in mind that a horse will be more comfort-able cantering on the right lead while it's turning to the right and it will feel better running to the left on the left lead.

As you begin to teach your horse to canter, don't focus on getting it to do any particular canter. Just let it get up to speed first, so it can learn what it feels like to canter with you on its back. Once the horse becomes comfortable with that, you can begin to focus on the correct canter. As you're teaching your horse to canter, which will probably be in a controlled setting (like an arena), keep in mind what direc-tion the horse will be traveling and cue it for that direction. For example, if the horse will be running toward the right, cue the horse to canter on the right lead. Again, don't be concerned about getting the *correct* canter at first. Although you aren't looking for a perfect canter, proper cueing will make it easier to perfect that at a later date.

The right and left canter are cued in the same way—you just switch sides. For a right canter, you want the right side of the horse to stretch out ahead of the left side, so as you look down while the horse canters, you should see the right shoulder slightly ahead of the left shoulder. To get that result, apply pressure to the right side. That pressure will cue the horse to move toward that direction. Your left foot should move back and tap the left side of the horse at the back of the rib cage, which will drive the horse forward. You should also notice that this leg movement will cause your hips to turn slightly. In the case of a right canter, your right hip should be slightly ahead of the left hip. In other words, your hips should be parallel with the horse's shoulders. This position for both horse and rider is essential to maintain balance while running and turning.

Some people suggest incorporating the reins into a canter cue. At a right canter, you'd apply very slight pressure to the left rein to hold that side back. That can help, but I think it's hard on the horse. When the horse is learning to run, I find it important to decrease any resistance to forward movement. Applying pressure to the head sends mixed messages to a young horse, and even if a horse knows how to canter well, I think resistance against that forward movement takes a toll on the overall balance. When that balance is lost, both horse and rider are more prone to accident, so I like to relax the reins as much as I can to let the horse be as comfortable and free to move as possible.

Of all the speeds, the canter is the hardest to teach, but not because it's overwhelmingly complex. It's because it can be scary. You are asking your horse to go faster, but not too fast, which tends to confuse the horse at first, and a confused horse tends to run, buck, and do other weird things—sometimes all at once. The main thing to do is to try to relax. A relaxed rider will react better to a horse's movements, so focus on what you're doing and try your best to relax.

The Gallop

The gallop is the last speed I'll be discussing. The gallop is the all-out speed, and because it's considerably faster than the others, I don't recommend attempting it until your horse is responsive to *all* our previous lessons. A gallop isn't the time to try to teach your horse how to turn properly.

The cue for a gallop is easy. From a trot or canter, lean forward slightly, apply pressure to the rib cage on both sides of the horse, and *hold on tight*. That's it. There's nothing complex about getting a horse up to that speed. Just let the horse have the reins and let it go! Give the horse as much rein as you can, so it can drop its head down and really stretch out. All *you* have to do is hold on.

Well, now you and your horse know the basics. You know how to walk, turn, stop, backup, trot, canter, and gallop. You now have the basic knowledge to train almost any other horse you'll come into contact with. Take the lessons you've learned and focus on perfecting your technique in a specific riding discipline, whether English or Western. The rest of the lessons in this book are meant to help fine tune your technique, and smooth out some of the rough spots.

27
CONTROLLING THE TURN

Horses sometimes like to second-guess their riders. They sometimes think that when you ask for a turn, what you really want is for them to turn in a complete circle. This isn't a huge problem, but it can be annoying. The best way I've found to fix this problem is to focus on a simple exercise, which is done by putting some traffic cones or feed buckets in a line, a few feet apart. Then ride the horse through the cones by turning it around each one. As you pass between the cones, stop the horse.

This exercise will benefit both you and the horse. It allows *you* a chance to practice your turning cues, and it gets the *horse* used to making partial turns. By moving the cones closer or farther apart, you can influence how tight a turn and how much forward movement the horse has to make. Throughout the lesson, focus on *control*. The turn is a place where you want to have things well under control.

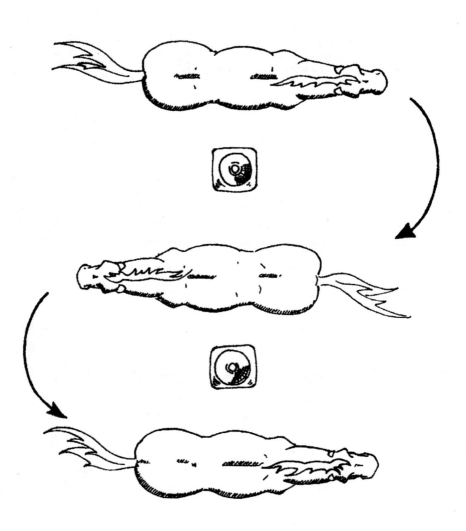

28

FEET/EYE COORDINATION

Going over logs is a great exercise. All you need to do is put some logs or fence posts on the ground and have your horse walk over them. Begin by walking over the logs while you walk in front of the horse, and then get on the horse and walk over the logs. Eventually, you should also be able to spread the logs out and have the horse trot over them.

This exercise forces the horse to pay attention to where its feet are. If you have a horse that routinely trips over objects when you're riding, this exercise will force it to focus on that problem, making the horse lift its legs better and watch where it puts its feet down. This exercise can also build stronger muscles. Because the horse has to lift up its legs and watch more closely, it will have to move its body more purposefully. Trotting over a series of logs will really help tone up your horse's legs and butt.

WALKING IN TIGHT SPOTS

Once you can walk over the logs, turn the logs and then walk between them. Make a maze with the logs and walk through it. Once you've gotten good at that, try *backing* through the maze. The idea is to get the horse used to walking narrow trails or bridges, or walking between two obstacles. Once you get good at the logs on the ground, raise them up higher, which will really get your horse ready for walking a narrow path between two objects.

DIFFERENT GROUND TYPES

Horses are often nervous about changes in terrain. For example, the change from gravel to grass can cause a horse great anxiety. To help your horse get over that, you want to teach it that you won't lead it into trouble. One way I do that is by getting the horse to walk over tarps of different textures and colors. Walking over tarps helps get a horse used to walking on new types of terrain—and even walking through water. Of course, the best way to get your horse used to walking on different terrains is by having it actually walk on those terrains, but tarps are a great way to get started. Like any exercise, it's best to start on the ground, leading the horse at first. After the horse can do it calmly while you're on the ground, you can climb aboard and try it while mounted.

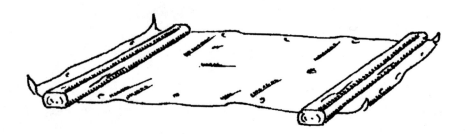

31

BRIDGES

My experience has shown that horses will either walk across a bridge right from the start or they'll avoid doing it at all costs. I can't remember ever working with a horse that was somewhere in between—so this lesson will either be easy or hard, depending on your horse. The principle is simple: build a fake bridge, using a few fence posts and a couple sheets of plywood. Then, once the bridge is made, walk the horse across it.

Of course, it may be easier said than done. Three things bother horses about bridges: the step up, the sound, and the step down.

Some bridges require a step up, so raise or lower your bridge to help your horse get used to the idea. If the horse can step over logs without a problem, you probably won't have much of a problem with the step up.

The sound is what really gets many horses. Bridges often make a hollow sound that seems to frighten some horses, and a frightened horse on a bridge can present a huge danger. There are many ways to get off a bridge, and a frightened horse might not choose the best way.

Even if the horse stays calm, it may not know how to step down off a bridge. Instead of stepping down, some horses jump down. That can be overcome with practice, but it's best to practice in a controlled setting.

A homemade bridge is a great way to safely train a horse to cross a real bridge.

32

MOUNTED FLAGGING

This is the last lesson in this book, but it's an important one. Think back to the original lesson about flagging. Flagging gets the horse used to having things move around it. Up to this point, you have been on the ground when you did this, but you aren't always going to be on the ground. You'll be in the saddle, which means you'll be in the horse's blind spot. This all comes together into one idea. When you're on the horse's back, it can't see you. But when you wave to a friend, point at something, swing a rope, or wear a scarf that billows in the wind, something is going to suddenly come into the horse's field of vision—and when that happens, your horse might not deal with it well.

Mounted flagging is meant to make the horse calm while things are moving around it when you're on its back. It's done just like it was done on the ground, but with a few twists. Don't do it only while the horse is standing still. Practice it while the horse is walking, too, or while it's turning in circles. Make the horse turn away from the flagging and then make it turn toward the flagging. Try it at a trot, then a canter. Try to do it as much as you can while you're mounted. In the long run, mounted flagging is one of the more important lessons in promoting safety.

I like to return to this lesson every now and then, no matter how much training a horse has been through. I've found that it's extremely beneficial for someone like me, who's always busy doing something else while I'm riding. Even if I'm just out on a trail ride with a friend, I tend to use my hands to emphasize whatever I'm talking about. A horse that can't handle my flailing limbs can be a nightmare to ride, so I practice this whenever I get the chance.

CONCLUSION

For each person, the concept of *horsemanship* means something different. For those of us who love horses and love working with horses, that meaning is deep inside of us. It's something that guides our lives—whether we like it or not. It's the thing that makes us choose a shirt with a horse on it at a store, or that prompts us to go to a movie with horses in it. It's a desire deep down inside of us that makes it a necessity for us to be around horses.

For me personally, it's a way of life. It's a choice I've made to do things that some people can only dream about. To ride a horse that's running with the wind is a feeling only a horseperson knows, and vastly different from riding a motorcycle or driving a car fast with the top down. When you're on the back of a horse, an animal that has the power to do whatever it wants, yet wants to run with you on its back—that's teamwork. To feel the wind in your face, to feel the horse beneath you, to lose track of everything else in your life, if only for a few seconds—that's freedom. That's why I ride horses. That's why I love working with horses. That's why I love the smell of horses on my clothes—it's the smell of *freedom*.

I sat down to write this book a long time ago. I put a lot of effort and thought into it. I didn't want to write just another book that gave a few out-of-order ideas about training horses. I wanted to write a book that you could use, from start to finish; a book that was easy to understand and follow. Most importantly, I wanted to write a book that would give any person the tools they'd need to discover the joy of working with horses. I hope I've given you some good ideas.

Now go out and work with your horse. Go out and try new ideas. Go out and *ride!*

Printed in the United States
51392LVS00005BA/195